Bible studies

Earl Grey with Ephesians

Advancing the Ministries of the Gospel

AMG *Publishers*

God's Word to you is our highest calling.

SANDRA GLAHN

Coffee Cup Bible Studies
Earl Grey with Ephesians

Published in association with
MacGregor and Luedeke Literary
P.O. Box 1316 Manzanita, OR 97130

ISBN: 978-1-61715-489-8

Editing and typesetting by Steele Editorial Services
(https://steeleeditorialservies.myportfolio.com)
with page design help from PerfecType, Nashville, Tennessee

Cover Design: Brian Woodlief at ImageWright Marketing and Design, Chattanooga, Tennessee

Printed in the United States of America

For Felicity, my Aussie friend, with fond memories
of Earl Grey afternoons

ACKNOWLEDGMENTS

No one who writes, particularly one who writes a Bible study, can possibly thank all the people who have influenced his or her work. If I were to try to do so, my list would be longer than the study itself. My mentors believed I could teach before I did, each opening doors to a variety of opportunities for me, for which I'm grateful. And my Washington Bible College and Dallas Theological Seminary professors all pointed out numerous truths from the biblical text.

Two essential elements in writing, however, are to be concise and to avoid boring the reader. So I will limit my thanks to the following: Thank you . . .

- Gary, my love, for being united with me in one purpose and consistently looking for ways to contribute to my flourishing.

- Angela Cirocco, my friend, for consistently and cheerfully providing scholarship, research and stories, as well as writing and editing assistance. Your partnership in this project has been invaluable.

- Biblical Studies Press (bible.org) and the translators of the NET Bible, apart from whom the Coffee Cup Bible Study series could be impossible. Thank you for laboring so others might grow in the Word.

INTRODUCTION TO THE
COFFEE CUP BIBLE STUDIES

"The precepts of the LORD are right, rejoicing the heart;
The commandment of the LORD is pure, enlightening the eyes."
(Psa. 19:8, NASB)

Congratulations! You have chosen wisely. By electing to study the Bible, you are choosing to spend time learning that which will rejoice the heart and enlighten the eyes. And while any study in the Bible is time well spent, the Coffee Cup Bible Studies series has some unique elements. So, before we get started, let's consider some of them to help you maximize your study time.

About coffee. You don't have to like coffee to use this series for regular Bible study. Tea works too—as the title *Earl Grey* suggests. So does milk. And water. Or no beverage at all. But embrace the beverage metaphor of taking a coffee break or gathering around the water cooler—a bit of downtime away from the routine, designed to refresh you. And you can imbibe alone, but you might enjoy the process even more with a group. More about that coming up.

Life rhythms. Most participants in Bible studies say they find it easier to keep up on weekdays than on the weekends, when their routine changes. For this reason, all Coffee Cup Bible Studies contain weekday Bible study questions that require active involvement, while the weekend segments (Saturdays and Sundays of each week) consist of short, passive readings that draw application from the texts you've been studying. Still, the specified days as laid out here serve as mere suggestions. Some people prefer to attend a Bible study one day and follow a four-day-per-week study schedule along with weekend readings. Others prefer to take twice as long to get through the book, cutting each day's selection roughly in half. Adapt the structure of days to fit your own needs.

Community. While you can complete this study individually, consider going through it with a few others. If you don't already belong to a Bible study group, find some friends and start one. Or connect periodically with others who organize short-term online groups. These vehicles give you opportunities to share what you're learning with a wider community and gain from their insights too. One U.S. reader told us she used Skype to have a regular Bible study using the series with a friend in Australia.

Aesthetics. At the author's Web site (aspire2.com), you will find links to art relating to studies in the Coffee Cup Bible Study series. For *Earl Grey with Ephesians* you'll discover fine arts with Ephesians tie-ins, links to other studies in Ephesians, recommended commentaries, and resource material. The more senses you can engage in your interaction with God's truth, the more you'll enjoy it and remember it.

Convenience. Rather than turning in your Bible to find the references, you'll find the entire text for each day included in this Coffee Cup Bible Studies book. While it's important to know your way around the Word, the series is designed this way so you can stash your study book in a purse, diaper bag, briefcase, or backpack, for use on the subway, at a coffee shop, or in a doctor's waiting room.

Why does the Coffee Cup series use the NET Bible translation? Accessible online from anywhere in the world, the NET (New English Translation) Bible is a contemporary translation from the ancient Greek, Hebrew, and Aramaic texts. A team of biblical language scholars volunteered to create it, because they shared a vision to make the Bible available worldwide without the high cost of permissions usually required for using copyrighted materials. Any other translation, with the exception of the King James Version, would have made the cost of including the Bible text prohibitive. Only through the generosity of Biblical Studies Press and the NET Bible translators is this convenience possible. For more information on this ministry, go to bible.org. (At bible.org you will also find numerous resources for Bible study and leadership training, including a special section for women in leadership.)

Sensitivity to time-and-culture considerations. When we study the Bible, in addition to observation, interpretation, and application, we must also consider three contexts: the past, the timeless, and the now. Many Bible studies skip the timeless (or theological) context. That is, they start by guiding readers to observe and interpret the words written to the original audience in the past (the exegetical step), but then they apply the words directly to themselves in their contemporary setting (the homiletical step). The result is sometimes misapplication. For example, in Ephesians 5 we read that Paul told slaves to obey their masters, so we might conclude that the author is endorsing the practice of slavery. Or we might think we need to obey our employers. Yet today's bosses don't own their employees, nor do they usually share the same household. Employment is by mutual agreement; slavery is not. So we should probably use the voluntary *respect* rather than obligatory *obey* when referring to an employment context. In the Coffee Cup series, our aim is to be particularly sensitive to the audience to whom the author's mail was addressed, but we also work to take the crucial step of separating what was intended for a limited audience from that which is for all audiences for all time.

Sensitivity to genre. Rather than crafting a series in which each study is laid out exactly like all the others, each Coffee Cup study is structured to best present the genre category we're examining—whether epistle or letter, poetry, Gospel, history, or narrative. The way we study an epistle, a letter sent to a group audience such as the Book of Ephesians, differs from how we might examine the compact poetry in Song of Songs or a prophetic work such as Malachi. That's why, while the studies in the Coffee Cup series may have similar elements, each study takes the approach to the text that best fits the genre. Whereas a prophetic work such as Malachi focuses less on exact terms and more on structural elements like God's question-and-answer test as laid out in that book's message, a study such as this one in Ephesians will include numerous word studies.

Selections for memorization. Nancy Writebol, a nurse with Samaritan's Purse who contracted the Ebola virus in Liberia, encourages believers to memorize Scripture. The virus affected her vision, making it nearly impossible for her to read. She would lie alone at night, crying out to God and wondering if she would survive. In those moments, she recalls, words of Scripture she had memorized ministered to her—phrases such as "even though I walk through the valley of the shadow of death, you are with me...." Many in the persecuted church tell of how the word hidden in their hearts ministers to them in their time of need. But even when we have easy access to the written word while driving in traffic, we can benefit from recalling, "A gentle answer turns away wrath, but a harsh word stirs up anger" (Prov. 15:1).

Whether we live where Christians endure persecution or materialism's pull tempts us toward apathy, we need God's Word in our hearts to help us stand strong in every situation. So, each week you'll find a verse or two to memorize.

Ready? If so, fasten your seat belt and fly back in time with me to the ancient Near East, where our journey begins.

INTRODUCTION TO
EARL GREY WITH EPHESIANS

When I visited Moscow as a married woman in my thirties, I noticed the women attending church services covered their hair. Not wanting to stand out, I put on a bandana. When I asked my host if I was wearing it correctly, she said, "They will understand because you are an American—but you honor yourself too much."

Honor? "How so?" I wondered aloud.

"Only women over sixty—the babushkas—wear such head coverings," she said. She held out her hand for me to give her my bandana. "Married women our age roll these into headbands." She took opposite corners, folded the cloth in half, and rolled from the middle.

I put on the "headband" and tied it at the nape of my neck.

She approved. "If you were unmarried, of course you would wear nothing on your head."

Clearly, in some places people can tell from a half-mile away whether a woman is married. In North America, wedding rings are more subtle—but they still communicate. And so do other such signs. For example, a BMW usually suggests a certain socio-economic status. And Jimmy Choo shoes suggest "fashionista." A toothless person begging on a street corner suggests another kind of lifestyle. Our externals may not always communicate accurately, but they definitely communicate.

In addition to these symbols, add the dynamic of honor. Today when the teen daughter of someone named Sarah Johnson misbehaves, that mom might tell her, "Start acting like a Johnson!" Such a statement acknowledges that one member can bring embarrassment to other members of their group. Sports fans know this all too well. Whenever the Washington Redskins beat the Dallas Cowboys, my brother-in-law often phones to humiliate our family. The loss of our team brings embarrassment . . . but usually only for one season.

In first-century Ephesus, people knew by the way women wore their hair whether they were maidens or married. By their clothing, people could tell if others were slaves, freed slaves, or freeborn. People could also tell with one glance if people were foreigners or citizens. And they could ascertain someone's approximate age and social class. Then, far more than now, people wore their identities. Multiply this symbol/honor/shame dynamic by ten, and you get the general idea about a cultural dynamic in the province of Asia at the time of the earliest Christians.

To people in such a context, Paul wrote the letter known to us as the Book of Ephesians. In the first half of his letter, he tells the believers who they are in Christ. Then, having established their identity, he devotes the second half to explaining how to live consistently with that identity, bringing honor to the Lord's great name.

The cultural dynamics may differ, but Paul's words have great application for us. Once we know who we are and whose we are, we are to live in light of these truths.

The backstory. A friend raised in a Christian home told me that he reached high school before he realized the Bible was not merely a book of motivational quotes. But in actuality, each verse fits within a context of one book that fits into a whole of sixty-six others comprised of numerous genres and written in different millennia. The total forms a united story of God's creation, humanity's fall, God's promise, redemption, and the coming restoration. One reason the Coffee Cup study books consider an entire Bible book or section of a book is to help readers see where verses fall in their original contexts and how they fit into the whole story.

God's big story begins with people in Eden, a death-free place of beautiful fellowship with their creator. These humans initially flourish according to plan. But they quickly choose to rebel. So, God in his mercy promises to send a redeemer who will come through a race descended from Abraham.

That redeemer is Jesus—"Emmanuel"—the savior who is "God with us." He willingly laid down his life for humanity's sins. Then he rose again and ascended to heaven, where he intercedes for his followers. He has promised to return to reign over the earth and ultimately to restore all of creation. But in the interim, he sends the Holy Spirit to indwell his followers—the church, his bride—and he has tasked her with the job of proclaiming the good news of his justice and love.

The Book of Ephesians provides instruction to the church, God's people, during this interim time before Christ returns. Through the apostle Paul, the Holy Spirit provides Jesus's followers with information about our new identity and how we should live in light of who we are.

Time and place.

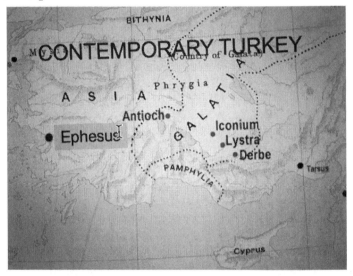

Location of Ancient Ephesus

Neither city nor harbor exists today on the site of ancient Ephesus. Although mentioned more than five hundred times in Greek literature alone, Ephesus has lain in ruins for more than five hundred years. The main reason for the city's demise: the Cayster River's silting of the Ephesian harbor and the resulting loss of trade.

At one time, however, Ephesus held a prominent position as the most important city in Ionian Asia Minor. At the height of the Roman Empire's power, the city was an important commercial center, third only behind Rome, Italy, and Alexandria, Egypt, having a population that ranged between a quarter- and a half-million people. From

Ephesus, Pompey released his soldiers, and Cleopatra and Mark Antony gathered their ships before waging the ill-fated battle at Actium.[1] According to the ancient philosopher and geographer Strabo, Ephesus was founded by Amazon women—a tribe of female warriors from central Eurasia.[2] The city's walls marked the end of the road from India, and its prime location on the Aegean Sea guaranteed its success as an international port lying at the gateway to Asia.

Ephesus was the legendary birthplace of the twin gods Artemis and Apollo[3] and home to Artemis's spectacular temple—the preeminent Wonder of the Ancient World. Artemis is the Greek persona of the Roman goddess Diana, goddess of the hunt. She is a confirmed virgin whom we usually see depicted with a bow and arrow and flanked by dogs or deer. But in Ephesus, her statue was covered with bulbous appendages, and she took on a special connection with midwifery.

Artemis's temple, in addition to its prominence as a pagan worship site, served as the General Depository of Asia. People came from all over the known world to bring their money for safekeeping.[4] The powerful goddess herself, it was believed, protected its assets. Temple guards added to the guarantee.

Although Shakespeare used the port of Ephesus as his setting for *The Comedy of Errors,* the city's history reads less like a comedy than as a tragedy, as its occupants were notorious for siding with the losers. Yet Ephesus escaped destruction time and again, because to ruin it would have meant slaughtering the cash cow.

The city's streets were crowded with statues, which—along with coins—provided the only way for those in the lower classes to see a ruler's face. Many statues came with removable heads, a handy feature in light of the often-rapid succession of emperors. Sculptures and temples bore bright colors, and many people found employment in keeping them freshly painted.

Despite its relative ease at the time, compared to contemporary standards, life in Ephesus was difficult. Girls married in their late teens. And Peter Brown writing in *The Body and Society* describes life expectancy empire-wide as being less than 25 years. "Of those surviv-

---

[1] In the past decade, Arsinoë's body has been identified. See Foggo, Daniel, "Found: the Sister Cleopatra Killed," *The Sunday Times,* March 15, 2009,

[2] Strabo, *Geography* 11.5.3–4; cf. 12.3.21

[3] *Ibid.* 14.1.21.

[4] See Julius Caesar's *Civil Wars 3.33* and *3.105.*

ing childhood," he writes, "only four out of every hundred men, and fewer women, lived beyond age fifty."[5] For population rates to have remained constant, each woman had to produce an average of five children.[6] The primary cause of death for men was war; for women, childbirth.

In 48 BC, Julius Caesar arrived in Alexandria and sided with Cleopatra in a faction against her remaining siblings. Her younger sister, Arsinoë, escaped, pulled together an army, and assumed the title of pharaoh. For her rebellion Caesar had Arsinoë taken to Rome, where he humiliated her as part of his triumph. Although generals had a habit of strangling prisoners after their glory-marches, Caesar opted to exile Arsinoë back in Ephesus in the Temple of Artemis. Mark Antony, doubtless under the influence of her sister Cleopatra, later ordered Arsinoë dragged from the temple and executed on its steps. Such a violation of the sacred temple, considered a place of refuge, outraged Ephesus's people.

Following Antony's and Cleopatra's deaths, Caesar Augustus reorganized the province, and in 29 BC he named Ephesus its administrative center. That made it the capital of the richest province—Asia. And the city began to be known as the "chief city of Asia."

The next major development in the city's history was religious. Mentioned in the New Testament (Acts 19), Ephesus served as home base to Paul of Tarsus for three years (c. A.D. 50–53). To or from Ephesus he probably wrote the New Testament epistles known to us as First Corinthians, First Timothy, and—of course—the Book of Ephesians.[7]

---

[5] Brown, Peter Robert Lamont. *The Body and Society: Men, Women, and Sexual Renunciation in Early Christianity.* New York: Columbia University Press, 1988: 6.

[6] *Ibid.,* 12–13.

[7] Though the words "to the Ephesians" don't appear in the earliest, most reputable manuscripts and one early list of Paul's epistles omits the letter to the Ephesians, this list does include an otherwise-unknown letter to the Laodiceans. As Asian Laodicea was near Ephesus, the epistle was probably intended for both Ephesus and Laodicea or for a group of several churches in Asia. Considering that Paul lived in Ephesus for about three years, it would be odd for him to omit personal greetings (cp. Romans 16) if he intended his missive only for the Ephesian community. This omission makes more sense if he sent his letter to more than one location.

The first mention of Ephesus in relation to the apostle Paul occurs in the Book of Acts, with the city mentioned four times in ten verses:

"They arrived at Ephesus, where Paul left Priscilla and Aquila [fellow Jews who shared his occupation of tent making]. He himself went into the synagogue and reasoned with the Jews. When they asked him to spend more time with them, he declined. But as he left, he promised, "I will come back if it is God's will." Then he set sail from Ephesus . . . . Meanwhile a Jew named Apollos, a native of Alexandria, came to Ephesus. He was a learned man, with a thorough knowledge of the Scriptures. He had been instructed in the way of the Lord, and he spoke with fervor in the Spirit and taught about Jesus accurately, though he knew only the baptism of John. He began to speak boldly in the synagogue. When Priscilla and Aquila heard him, they invited him to their home and explained to him the way of God more adequately. When Apollos wanted to go to Achaia, the brothers encouraged him and wrote to the disciples there to welcome him. . . . While Apollos was at Corinth, Paul took the road through the interior and arrived at Ephesus (Acts 18:19–19:1).

As mentioned, Ephesus would serve as home base to Paul for three years. He taught daily in a place called the Hall of Tyranus (Acts 20:31), the location of which has yet to be discovered. From his base at the seaport, Paul launched a mission into the entire province of Asia. After a trip through Galatia, he wrote an epistle, "The Epistle to the Galatians," back to his friends there, probably during the winter of A.D. 52–53.

The amphitheater where the Ephesian disturbance took place still stands.

The reputation of Ephesus for occult magic is referenced both in the Bible and in other literature. Apparently, a number of Christian converts who had practiced sorcery brought their magic books and burned a valuable stash of them in plain sight. This bold move happened in a context where Artemis of the Ephesians was considered the master of the astrological world. Ephesian statues of Artemis dating to this period have signs of the zodiac displayed prominently below her necklace. A statue of Hecate, the goddess of the underworld, stood in her temple. And some think that the trunk areas on Artemis statues are covered with animals because she prevailed over the earthly realm, which included human and beast.

Ephesus was a center of commerce for people trafficking in the supernatural. Magicians charged exorbitant prices for love potions. And people would pay large sums to create curses using a combination of what was known as the "Ephesian letters"—likely individual letters on dice that people would throw to create combinations for magical spells.[8]

After the magic-book bonfire, Paul determined to go to Rome, so he sent two of his helpers, including Timothy, ahead of him to Macedonia. About that time, the writer of Acts records that an event occurred in Ephesus which brought together Jewish, Christian and pagan forces.

A silversmith who profited by making shrines of Artemis called together his tradesmen and warned them that Paul was leading astray many throughout the province of Asia. Because Paul was teaching that man-made gods were not real gods, the trade workers were scared their occupation would lose its reputation, and the temple of Artemis would be discredited.

Fearing economic ruin, the people of the city seized Paul's companions from Macedonia and rushed into the theater. Paul's disciples and high-ranking friends held him back from entering, and instead, as the author of Acts says, "The Jews pushed Alexander to the front, and some of the crowd shouted instructions to him. He motioned for silence in order to make a defense before the people. But when they realized he was a Jew, they all shouted in unison for about two hours: 'Great is Artemis of the Ephesians!' "

After quieting the crowd, the city clerk asked the people, "Doesn't all the world know that the city of Ephesus is the guardian of the

---

[8] Arnold, C. E. Ephesians: *Power and Magic*. Grand Rapids: Baker Academic, 1992.

temple of the great Artemis and of her image, which fell from heaven? Therefore, since these facts are undeniable, you ought to be quiet and not do anything rash." He urged them to take up their objection in the courts, warning "we are in danger of being charged with rioting" (Acts 19:24–20:1). Shortly after that, Paul set out for Macedonia, and sometime later Timothy returned to take his place in Ephesus. After the apostle's departure, perhaps up to four years later, he wrote an epistle intended for circulation in Asia. And we know this epistle as the Book of Ephesians. Tradition says Paul wrote it as a circular letter (one intended for believers in several cities, not just Ephesus) from a prison in Rome between A.D. 59 and 61.

A decade or two later, a couple of major events happened outside of Ephesus that would have likely affected the city. The first was the fall of Jerusalem, of particular grief for the Jews scattered abroad. (Although archaeologists have yet to find a synagogue, a menorah inscribed in stone on the second-century library steps provides evidence that Jews lived in Ephesus in the first century.[9]) The other event is the destruction of many port cities such as Pompeii and Herculaneum at the base of Mt. Vesuvius, which erupted in A.D. 79. These cities would have had ships that sailed to and from Ephesus.

Priscilla and Aquila, Paul's business and ministry partners, initially moved to Corinth sometime after Claudius expelled the Jews from Rome,[10] and eventually the couple accompanied Paul to Ephesus.[11] Also, tradition places Jesus's mother, Mary, in Ephesus along with the elderly John the Apostle after his exile on Patmos in the 90s. And John reportedly wrote the Gospel of John in Ephesus, which also served as a strategic base for evangelizing Europe. Timothy continued to minister in the city after Paul left.[12]

Ignatius (A.D. 35–108), bishop of Antioch, wrote seven letters while guards marched him across Asia Minor to face the lions in Rome. One such missive was addressed to the Ephesian church. In it he drew on his knowledge of a familiar public procession of dressed-up Artemis statues carried from one city gate to the other. And Ignatius

---

[9] Paul Trebilco in *The Early Christians in Ephesus from Paul to Ignatius* (Grand Rapids, Mich., Wm. B. Eerdman's, 2007) explores at length the evidence of a Jewish population.

[10] Acts 18:2

[11] Acts 18:19

[12] 1 Timothy 1:3

ascribed to their actions Christian meaning. His writings give us some of the few hints we have about the rites of the Artemis cult.

The decline that eventually turned Ephesus into a ghost town happened gradually. I've mentioned the harbor silting. But also, an earthquake in the second century A.D. buried terrace houses in a mudslide—a disaster for its occupants, but a goldmine for contemporary archaeologists. Their work provides historical details that benefit our understanding of New Testament backgrounds.

In 262, Goths plundered the temple of Artemis and burned it. Still, after Constantinople, Ephesus was the most important city in Asia during the Byzantine Era, hosting Christianity's third Ecumenical Council in 431.

Crippled by its lack of access to the Aegean's waters (essential to trade), the city changed rulers many times in the centuries that followed, and gradually dwindled to nothing. Today its ruins lie near the town of Kuşadasi, not far from Izmir in modern-day Turkey.

Archaeologists estimate that they have unearthed only about 10 to 20 percent of Ephesus's treasures. Even so, a theater, odeon, library, streets lined with columns, terrace houses, sculptures, coins, and much more, provide a virtual historical and archaeological playground for researchers and tourists alike. Among marble, frescoes, and mosaics, visitors can imagine life as it once was in this political, cultural, and religious center of the ancient Mediterranean, the one-time jewel in the crown of the wealthiest province of the Roman Empire.

CONTENTS

WEEK 1 OF 6

United: Ephesians 1

SUNDAY: I WILL ALWAYS LOVE YOU

Do a search of break-up songs, and you'll find a long list. Most such songs are about romance—and there are plenty of them. But not every break-up that happens is between romantic partners. Think of parents estranged from children. Siblings who refuse to speak to each other. Business partners who sue one another. Bosses and employees who once liked each other but who later can't stand to inhabit the same room. We humans constantly endure relationships in which someone has "lost that loving feeling."

The Ephesians were no different. We find them mentioned several places in scripture. In a message sent through a vision Christ gave to John, the Lord rebuked the Ephesians for departing from their first love (Rev. 2:1–7). His exhortation? Not to "return to your former affection," as we might expect, but to repent and return to their former works.

Christ assessed the Ephesians' love by their actions, gauging their loyalty by whether they did the works they had done at first. Maybe they still hated false teaching, but they shrugged at idolatry.

We don't worship the same idols that were present in Ephesus; the desire to hang out in the temple of Artemis doesn't exactly make our "temptations" list. Yet we still have our idols—our list of stuff we prioritize above God. Perhaps we waste hours on the computer while claiming we can't fit Bible-reading into our schedules. Or the thought of praying slips our minds because we depend on our own ingenuity to get us out of messes. Or we lack gratitude because we fail to see the hand of providence. Or we recite lyrics verbatim, yet we insist we never were good at hiding God's word in our hearts. Or we cling to material goods while our brothers and sisters who live in poverty ask, "Why isn't our rich family helping to care for us?" Maybe it's the grudge we nurse. The tongue we won't control. Our loyalty to political party over the gospel. Our anger at God when he withholds what we think is best. Or our endless pursuit of food, books, careers, shopping, respect from others, love. . . . What's the solution? Twice Jesus tells the Ephesians, "Repent." And His vision of repenting goes far beyond merely mumbling "my bad." True repentance means, by His power, "doing a 180," making a radical change, agreeing with God, finding accountability in community, and getting serious about throwing out the enemy and slamming the door. Our love for God ultimately shows itself in actions. Simply put, true love can't help but show itself in loving acts.

Often in the early stages of our relationship with Christ, we act like new brides, delirious with joy over our grooms. But then God's people wound us. Or God seems silent. Circumstances overwhelm us. We grow weary. And jaded. We might even roll our eyes when we see new believers' enthusiasm.

Like the Ephesians, we may need to repent and return to our former works. Think about the works a fiancée does. Her love and affection show in her deeds, in how she talks about her guy . . . in the notes she sends, and in the gifts she buys or makes. If she loves her man, nobody has to tell her to avoid flirting with other guys. Her actions reveal her heart. Her loyalties make themselves known.

What do your actions say about your love and loyalties? Whom do you love? Is it the one who has promised He will always love you?

Revelation 2:4-5: "But I have this against you: You have departed from your first love! Therefore, remember from what high state you have fallen and repent! Do the deeds you did at the first; if not, I will come to you and remove your lampstand from its place—that is, if you do not repent"

Prayer: *Lord Jesus, forgive my lack of love for you. I love you imperfectly, but I do love you. Help me to live out that reality through a deeper repentance, a horror of sin, and a dread of its approach. Help me to guard my heart as a place for you first in all things. Grant me deeper power in private prayer, more sweetness in Your Word, a more steadfast grip on its truth, a truer loyalty to You, and a more sacrificial love for Your people. Help me to show my love for You by how I care for Your image-bearers and how I spend my energy. In Jesus' name, Amen.*

MONDAY: WHO AM I? WHY AM I HERE?

1. Pray and ask God to give you understanding and insight. Then read the apostle Paul's letter to the Ephesians (included below, from the NET Bible) in one sitting. As you read, notice how the first half emphasizes what God has done for us and the second half emphasizes who we should be as a result. Underline references to what Christ has done for those who believe in him. FYI, boldface type on verses is original to the NET translation; the bold flags places where Paul is referencing the Old Testament.

> **Ephesians 1:1** From Paul, an apostle of Christ Jesus by the will of God, to the saints [in Ephesus], the faithful in Christ Jesus. **1:2** Grace and peace to you from God our Father and the Lord Jesus Christ! **1:3** Blessed is the God and Father of our Lord Jesus Christ, who has blessed us with every spiritual blessing in the heavenly realms in Christ. **1:4** For he chose us in Christ before the foundation of the world that we may be holy and unblemished in his sight in love. **1:5** He did this by predestining us to adoption as his sons through Jesus Christ, according to the pleasure of his will—**1:6** to the praise of the glory of his grace that he has freely bestowed on us in his dearly loved Son. **1:7** In him we have redemption through his blood, the forgiveness of our trespasses, according to the riches of his grace **1:8** that he lavished on us in all wisdom and insight. **1:9** He did this when he revealed to us the secret of his will, according to his good pleasure that he set forth in Christ, **1:10** toward the administration of the fullness of the times, to head up all things in Christ—the things in heaven and the things on earth. **1:11** In Christ we too have been claimed as God's own possession, since we were predestined according to the one purpose of him who accomplishes all things according to the counsel of his will **1:12** so that we, who were the first to set our hope on Christ, would be to

the praise of his glory. **1:13** And when you heard the word of truth (the gospel of your salvation)—when you believed in Christ—you were marked with the seal of the promised Holy Spirit, **1:14** who is the down payment of our inheritance, until the redemption of God's own possession, to the praise of his glory.

1:15 For this reason, because I have heard of your faith in the Lord Jesus and your love for all the saints, **1:16** I do not cease to give thanks for you when I remember you in my prayers. **1:17** I pray that the God of our Lord Jesus Christ, the Father of glory, may give you spiritual wisdom and revelation in your growing knowledge of him, **1:18**—since the eyes of your heart have been enlightened—so that you may know what is the hope of his calling, what is the wealth of his glorious inheritance in the saints, **1:19** and what is the incomparable greatness of his power toward us who believe, as displayed in the exercise of his immense strength. **1:20** This power he exercised in Christ when he raised him from the dead and seated him at his right hand in the heavenly realms **1:21** far above every rule and authority and power and dominion and every name that is named, not only in this age but also in the one to come. **1:22** And God **put all things under** Christ's **feet,** and he gave him to the church as head over all things. **1:23** Now the church is his body, the fullness of him who fills all in all.

Ephesians 2:1 And although you were dead in your transgressions and sins, **2:2** in which you formerly lived according to this world's present path, according to the ruler of the kingdom of the air, the ruler of the spirit that is now energizing the sons of disobedience, **2:3** among whom all of us also formerly lived out our lives in the cravings of our flesh, indulging the desires of the flesh and the mind, and were by nature children of wrath even as the rest...

2:4 But God, being rich in mercy, because of his great love with which he loved us, **2:5** even though we were dead in transgressions, made us alive together with Christ—by grace you are saved!—**2:6** and he raised us up with him and seated us with him in the heavenly realms in Christ Jesus, **2:7** to demonstrate in the coming ages the surpassing wealth of his grace in kindness toward us in Christ Jesus. **2:8** For by grace you are saved through faith, and this is not from yourselves, it is the gift of God; **2:9** it is not from works, so that no one can boast. **2:10** For we are his workmanship, having been created in Christ Jesus for good works that God prepared beforehand so we may do them.

2:11 Therefore remember that formerly you, the Gentiles in the flesh—who are called "uncircumcision" by the so-called "circumcision" that is performed on the body by human hands— **2:12** that you were at that time without the Messiah, alienated from the citizenship of Israel and strangers to the covenants of promise, having no hope and without God in the world. **2:13** But now in Christ Jesus you who used to be far away have been brought near by the blood of Christ. **2:14** For he is our peace, the one who made both groups into one and who destroyed the middle wall of partition, the hostility, **2:15** when he nullified in his flesh the law of commandments in decrees. He did this to create in himself one new man out of two, thus making peace, **2:16** and to reconcile them both in one body to God through the cross, by which the hostility has been killed. **2:17** And he came and preached peace to you who were far off and peace to those who were near, **2:18** so that through him we both have access in one Spirit to the Father. **2:19** So then you are no longer foreigners and noncitizens, but you are fellow citizens with the saints and members of God's household, **2:20** because you have been built on the foundation of the apostles and prophets, with Christ Jesus himself as the cornerstone. **2:21** In him the whole building, being joined together, grows into a holy temple in the Lord, **2:22** in whom you also are being built together into a dwelling place of God in the Spirit.

Ephesians 3:1 For this reason I, Paul, the prisoner of Christ Jesus for the sake of you Gentiles—**3:2** if indeed you have heard of the stewardship of God's grace that was given to me for you, **3:3** that by revelation the divine secret was made known to me, as I wrote before briefly. **3:4** When reading this, you will be able to understand my insight into this secret of Christ. **3:5** Now this secret was not disclosed to people in former generations as it has now been revealed to his holy apostles and prophets by the Spirit, **3:6** namely, that through the gospel the Gentiles are fellow heirs, fellow members of the body, and fellow partakers of the promise in Christ Jesus. **3:7** I became a servant of this gospel according to the gift of God's grace that was given to me by the exercise of his power. **3:8** To me—less than the least of all the saints—this grace was given, to proclaim to the Gentiles the unfathomable riches of Christ **3:9** and to enlighten everyone about God's secret plan—a secret that has been hidden for ages in God who has created all things. **3:10** The purpose of this enlightenment is that through the church the multifaceted wisdom of God should now be disclosed to the rulers and the authorities in the heavenly realms. **3:11** This was according to the eternal purpose that he accomplished in Christ Jesus our Lord, **3:12** in whom we have boldness and confident access to God because of Christ's faithfulness. **3:13** For this reason

I ask you not to lose heart because of what I am suffering for you, which is your glory.

3:14 For this reason I kneel before the Father, **3:15** from whom every family in heaven and on the earth is named. **3:16** I pray that according to the wealth of his glory he may grant you to be strengthened with power through his Spirit in the inner person, **3:17** that Christ may dwell in your hearts through faith, so that, because you have been rooted and grounded in love, **3:18** you may be able to comprehend with all the saints what is the breadth and length and height and depth, **3:19** and thus to know the love of Christ that surpasses knowledge, so that you may be filled up to all the fullness of God.

3:20 Now to him who by the power that is working within us is able to do far beyond all that we ask or think, **3:21** to him be the glory in the church and in Christ Jesus to all generations, forever and ever. Amen.

Ephesians 4:1 I, therefore, the prisoner for the Lord, urge you to live worthily of the calling with which you have been called, **4:2** with all humility and gentleness, with patience, bearing with one another in love, **4:3** making every effort to keep the unity of the Spirit in the bond of peace. **4:4** There is one body and one Spirit, just as you too were called to the one hope of your calling, **4:5** one Lord, one faith, one baptism, **4:6** one God and Father of all, who is over all and through all and in all.

4:7 But to each one of us grace was given according to the measure of the gift of Christ. **4:8** Therefore it says, **"When he ascended on high he captured captives; he gave gifts to men."** **4:9** Now what is the meaning of **"he ascended,"** except that he also descended to the lower regions, namely, the earth? **4:10** He, the very one who descended, is also the one who ascended above all the heavens, in order to fill all things. **4:11** It was he who gave some as apostles, some as prophets, some as evangelists, and some as pastors and teachers, **4:12** to equip the saints for the work of ministry, that is, to build up the body of Christ, **4:13** until we all attain to the unity of the faith and of the knowledge of the Son of God—a mature person, attaining to the measure of Christ's full stature. **4:14** So we are no longer to be children, tossed back and forth by waves and carried about by every wind of teaching by the trickery of people who craftily carry out their deceitful schemes. **4:15** But practicing the truth in love, we will in all things grow up into Christ, who is the head. **4:16** From him the whole body grows, fitted and held together through every supporting ligament. As each one does its part, the body grows in love.

4:17 So I say this, and insist in the Lord, that you no longer live as the Gentiles do, in the futility of their thinking. **4:18** They are darkened in their understanding, being alienated from the life of God because of the ignorance that is in them due to the hardness of their hearts. **4:19** Because they are callous, they have given themselves over to indecency for the practice of every kind of impurity with greediness. **4:20** But you did not learn about Christ like this, **4:21** if indeed you heard about him and were taught in him, just as the truth is in Jesus. **4:22** You were taught with reference to your former way of life to lay aside the old man who is being corrupted in accordance with deceitful desires, **4:23** to be renewed in the spirit of your mind, **4:24** and to put on the new man who has been created in God's image—in righteousness and holiness that comes from truth.

4:25 Therefore, having laid aside falsehood, **each one of you speak the truth with his neighbor,** for we are members of one another. **4:26 Be angry and do not sin**; do not let the sun go down on the cause of your anger. **4:27** Do not give the devil an opportunity. **4:28** The one who steals must steal no longer; rather he must labor, doing good with his own hands, so that he may have something to share with the one who has need. **4:29** You must let no unwholesome word come out of your mouth, but only what is beneficial for the building up of the one in need, that it may give grace to those who hear. **4:30** And do not grieve the Holy Spirit of God, by whom you were sealed for the day of redemption. **4:31** You must put away all bitterness, anger, wrath, quarreling, and slanderous talk—indeed all malice. **4:32** Instead, be kind to one another, compassionate, forgiving one another, just as God in Christ also forgave you.

Ephesians 5:1 Therefore, be imitators of God as dearly loved children **5:2** and live in love, just as Christ also loved us and gave himself for us, a sacrificial and fragrant offering to God. **5:3** But among you there must not be either sexual immorality, impurity of any kind, or greed, as these are not fitting for the saints. **5:4** Neither should there be vulgar speech, foolish talk, or coarse jesting—all of which are out of character—but rather thanksgiving. **5:5** For you can be confident of this one thing: that no person who is immoral, impure, or greedy (such a person is an idolater) has any inheritance in the kingdom of Christ and God.

5:6 Let nobody deceive you with empty words, for because of these things God's wrath comes on the sons of disobedience. **5:7** Therefore do not be partakers with them, **5:8** for you were at one time darkness, but now you are light in the Lord. Walk as children of the light—**5:9** for the fruit of the light consists in all goodness, righteousness, and truth—**5:10** trying to learn what is pleasing to the Lord. **5:11** Do not participate in the unfruitful deeds of darkness, but rather expose them. **5:12** For the things they do in secret are shameful even to mention. **5:13** But all things being exposed by the light are made evident. **5:14** For everything made evident is light, and for this reason it says:

> "Awake, O sleeper!
> Rise from the dead,
> and Christ will shine on you!"

5:15 Therefore be very careful how you live—not as unwise but as wise, **5:16** taking advantage of every opportunity, because the days are evil. **5:17** For this reason do not be foolish, but be wise by understanding what the Lord's will is. **5:18** And do not get drunk with wine, which is debauchery, but be filled by the Spirit, **5:19** speaking to one another in psalms, hymns, and spiritual songs, singing and making music in your hearts to the Lord, **5:20** always giving thanks to God the Father for each other in the name of our Lord Jesus Christ, **5:21** and submitting to one another out of reverence for Christ.

5:22 Wives, submit to your husbands as to the Lord, **5:23** because the husband is the head of the wife as also Christ is the head of the church—he himself being the savior of the body. **5:24** But as the church submits to Christ, so also wives should submit to their husbands in everything. **5:25** Husbands, love your wives just as Christ loved the church and gave himself for her **5:26** to sanctify her by cleansing her with the washing of the water by the word, **5:27** so that he may present the church to himself as glorious—not having a stain or wrinkle, or any such blemish, but holy and blameless. **5:28** In the same way husbands ought to love their wives as their own bodies. He who loves his wife loves himself. **5:29** For no one has ever hated his own body but he feeds it and takes care of it, just as Christ also does the church, **5:30** for we are members of his body. **5:31 For this reason a man will leave his father and mother and will be joined to his wife, and the two will become one flesh. 5:32** This mystery is great—but I am actually speaking with reference to Christ and the church. **5:33** Nevertheless, each one of you must also love his own wife as he loves himself, and the wife must respect her husband.

Ephesians 6:1 Children, obey your parents in the Lord for this is right. **6:2 "Honor your father and mother,"** which is the first commandment accompanied by a promise, namely, **6:3 "that it may go well with you and that you will live a long time on the earth."**

6:4 Fathers, do not provoke your children to anger, but raise them up in the discipline and instruction of the Lord.

6:5 Slaves, obey your human masters with fear and trembling, in the sincerity of your heart as to Christ, **6:6** not like those who do their work only when someone is watching—as people-pleasers—but as slaves of Christ doing the will of God from the heart. **6:7** Obey with enthusiasm, as though serving the Lord and not people, **6:8** because you know that each person, whether slave or free, if he does something good, this will be rewarded by the Lord.

6:9 Masters, treat your slaves the same way, giving up the use of threats, because you know that both you and they have the same master in heaven, and there is no favoritism with him.

6:10 Finally, be strengthened in the Lord and in the strength of his power. **6:11** Clothe yourselves with the full armor of God so that you may be able to stand against the schemes of the devil. **6:12** For our struggle is not against flesh and blood, but against the rulers, against the powers, against the world rulers of this darkness, against the spiritual forces of evil in the heavens. **6:13** For this reason, take up the full armor of God so that you may be able to stand your ground on the evil day, and having done everything, to stand. **6:14** Stand firm therefore, by fastening the belt of truth around your waist, by putting on the breastplate of righteousness, **6:15** by fitting your feet with the preparation that comes from the good news of peace, **6:16** and in all of this, by taking up the shield of faith with which you can extinguish all the flaming arrows of the evil one. **6:17** And take the **helmet of salvation** and the sword of the Spirit, which is the word of God. **6:18** With every prayer and petition, pray at all times in the Spirit, and to this end be alert, with all perseverance and requests for all the saints. **6:19** Pray for me also, that I may be given the message when I begin to speak—that I may confidently make known the mystery of the gospel, **6:20** for which I am an ambassador in chains. Pray that I may be able to speak boldly as I ought to speak.

6:21 Tychicus, my dear brother and faithful servant in the Lord, will make everything known to you, so that you too may know about my circumstances, how I am doing. **6:22** I have sent him to you for this very purpose, that you may know our circumstances and that he may encourage your hearts.

6:23 Peace to the brothers and sisters, and love with faith, from God the Father and the Lord Jesus Christ. **6:24** Grace be with all of those who love our Lord Jesus Christ with an undying love.

1. What stood out to you as you read?

_____

_____

Tuesday: United

1. Read the apostle Paul's salutation, and notice what title he gives himself:

> "From Paul, an apostle of Christ Jesus by the will of God, to the saints [in Ephesus], the faithful in Christ Jesus. Grace and peace to you from God our Father and the Lord Jesus Christ!" (vv. 1–2).

"Apostle" (vs. 1)—Paul describes himself as "an apostle of Christ Jesus by the will of God." Why would he feel the need to begin with such credentials?

The word "apostle" comes from the Greek *apostolos,* meaning "sent one." In the narrowest use of the word in the Bible, an apostle was one of "the twelve" chosen by Jesus and specifically sent out by him (like Peter, James, John). The original twelve apostles included Judas, the betrayer of Jesus, and after Judas's death he was replaced to keep the number at twelve. In the Book of Acts we read Peter's description of the qualifications required of the person to replace Judas: "Of the men who have accompanied us all the time that the Lord Jesus went in and out among us—beginning with the baptism of John, until the day that He was taken up from us—one of these must become a witness with us of His resurrection" (Acts 1:21–22, NASB). The group cast lots, and Matthias became Judas's replacement.

Yet sometimes in the New Testament, the title "apostle" refers to people other than the twelve. In fact, it's possible that the spiritual gift of apostle (see Eph. 4:11) is the equivalent to what we might today refer to as "missionary" and "church planter." Paul describes Andronicus and Junia as being known "among the apostles" (Rom. 16:7). One of the church fathers, John Chrysostom (A.D. 349–407), wrote about Junia, "O how great is the devotion of this woman [Junia] that she should be counted worthy of the appellation of apostle!" Additionally, people in the early church described Mary Magdalene as "apostle to the apostles," because she announced the good news to the Twelve that Jesus was alive. People gave her this title because the angel at Jesus' empty tomb "sent" her to go tell the disciples Christ had risen.

As the author of Ephesians, Paul was not one of the twelve disciples who lived daily with Jesus on earth, nor did he see Jesus before the resurrection. But Paul did encounter the risen Christ while on his way to Damascus, Syria (you can read the story in Acts 9:1–22). There God renamed him from the Jewish "Saul" to a name more familiar to the Gentiles of whom Paul would be "sent" to evangelize.

When Paul greets his readers in his letters, he usually reminds them of this God-ordained calling:

> **Romans 1:1: From Paul, a slave of Christ Jesus, called to be an apostle, set apart for the gospel of God . . .**
>
> **1 Corinthians 1:1: From Paul, called to be an apostle of Christ Jesus by the will of God . . .**
>
> **2 Corinthians 1:1: From Paul, an apostle of Christ Jesus by the will of God . . .**
>
> **Galatians 1:1: From Paul, an apostle (not from men, nor by human agency, but by Jesus Christ and God the Father who raised him from the dead) . . .**
>
> **Colossians 1:1: From Paul, an apostle of Christ Jesus by the will of God . . .**
>
> **1 Timothy 1:1: From Paul, an apostle of Christ Jesus by the command of God our Savior and of Christ Jesus our hope . . .**
>
> **Titus 1:1: From Paul, a slave of God and apostle of Jesus Christ ...**

Doubtless Paul referred to himself as an apostle in his introduction to Ephesians to remind his readers of his God-given authority in the mission. To be an apostle was to deliver the authoritative message of God. Thus, when Paul referred to himself as an apostle, he was reminding his readers that his message came ultimately from God. Paul wrote to his recipients in obedience to God, and his words carried Spirit-given authority.

2. Paul addresses his letter "to the saints" (1:1). When we hear the word "saint," many of us think of St. Patrick or St. Valentine or St. Joan of Arc. We might even think of St. Jerome. Or St. Mother Teresa. To many, saints make up a class of ultra-spiritual people. Yet that is actually not how the New Testament writers used the word—and they used it a lot (229 times in the Greek, to be exact). "Saint" is actually what New Testament writers call all who have believed in Christ. It is an identity marker, not a description of our works. Although we are all sinners, God has declared as "holy" those who have trusted Christ's payment on the cross for all their sins. Those of us who have done so are indwelt by the Holy Spirit of God. So, although we saints are imperfect, we have been declared righteous by the finished work of Christ. The title "saint," then, is a word that describes our position before God, if we have come to know him. Have you trusted in Christ alone to save you from your sins?

If so, write your name as "Saint _____."

3. Re-read chapter one and circle every time the phrase "in Christ" appears in the text.

Ephesians 1:1 From Paul, an apostle of Christ Jesus by the will of God, to the saints [in Ephesus], the faithful in Christ Jesus. **1:2** Grace and peace to you from God our Father and the Lord Jesus Christ!

1:3 Blessed is the God and Father of our Lord Jesus Christ, who has blessed us with every spiritual blessing in the heavenly realms in Christ. **1:4** For he chose us in Christ before the foundation of the world that we may be holy and unblemished in his sight in love. **1:5** He did this by predestining us to adoption as his sons through Jesus Christ, according to the pleasure of his will—**1:6** to the praise of the glory of his grace that he has freely bestowed on us in his dearly loved Son. **1:7** In him we have redemption through his blood, the forgiveness of our trespasses, according to the riches of his grace **1:8** that he lavished on us in all wisdom and insight. **1:9** He did this when he revealed to us the secret of his will, according to his good pleasure that he set forth in Christ, **1:10** toward the administration of the fullness of the times, to head up all things in Christ—the things in heaven and the things on earth. **1:11** In Christ we too have been claimed as God's own possession, since we were predestined according to the one purpose of him who accomplishes all things according to the counsel of his will **1:12** so that we, who were the first to set our hope on Christ, would be to the praise of his glory. **1:13** And when you heard the word of truth (the gospel of your salvation)—when you believed in Christ—you were marked with the seal of the promised Holy Spirit, **1:14** who is the down payment of our inheritance, until the redemption of God's own possession, to the praise of his glory.

1:15 For this reason, because I have heard of your faith in the Lord Jesus and your love for all the saints, **1:16** I do not cease to give thanks for you when I remember you in my prayers. **1:17** I pray that the God of our Lord Jesus Christ, the Father of glory, may give you spiritual wisdom and revelation in your growing knowledge of him, **1:18**—since the eyes of your heart have been enlightened—so that you may know what is the hope of his calling, what is the wealth of his glorious inheritance in the saints, **1:19** and what is the incomparable greatness of his power toward us who believe, as displayed in the exercise of his immense strength. **1:20** This power he exercised in Christ when he raised him from the dead and seated him at his right hand in the heavenly realms **1:21** far above every rule and authority and power and dominion and every name that is named, not only in this age but also in the one to come. **1:22** And God put all things under Christ's feet, and he gave him to the church as head over all things. **1:23** Now the church is his body, the fullness of him who fills all in all.

"In Christ" (1:1, 3, 4, 9, 10,11, 13, 20)—A brief survey of Paul's letters reveals that he closely connects a believer's state of salvation with that person's participation with Christ. Those who are "in Christ" have received the free gift of eternal life, but that life is not only a future benefit in heaven. Eternal life begins immediately at salvation. It is a state of being, not connected with a place. And being "in Christ" means that the one who believes in Jesus Christ participates in Christ's life and is being transformed into His image and likeness.

4. Where do the saints to whom Paul is writing appear to live (v. 1)?

In Ephesus

Does your Bible have the words "in Ephesus" in italics or brackets in Ephesians 1:1? If so, it's to indicate a translation issue with this phrase. The earliest and best manuscripts actually vary on what's written here. There are two reasons to suspect Paul's original letter did not actually specify the city. First, the earliest manuscripts don't include the words "in Ephesus." And second, the epistle itself does not include any greetings or city-specific information. In Paul's letter to the Romans, especially the last chapter, he greets many people he knows in Rome, yet in Ephesians he sends no specific greetings to inhabitants of Ephesus. This is especially surprising, since he lived and ministered there for three years (see Acts 20:31).

Have you ever received a letter in which you knew the "name field" changed for each recipient—where "Dear Angela" or "Dear Joe" was personalized for each recipient? Many think that sort of thing was what Paul intended with this epistle—to be a circular letter making the rounds to churches in Asia. If so, each church would have filled in the name of their own city.

We have some evidence that this may have been the case. About AD 140, Marcion, the son of an early bishop, created a list of early Christian writings. The letter to the Ephesians is absent in Marcion's list. Yet he did list a letter to the church at Laodicea—which is a little less than one hundred miles from Ephesus. No copies of a letter to Laodicea exist—unless "Ephesians" and Marcion's "Laodicea" are the same epistle. We know of Paul's interest in the church at Laodicea, because he mentioned it three times in his letter to the Colossians (4:13, 15, 16), in one instance telling those in Colossae to read the letter he sent to Laodicea. So, it's entirely possible this letter went to several locations in the province of Asia (modern Turkey).

By the way, the text variants between older and more recent manuscripts, such as phrases like "in Ephesus" are not anything to split hairs over. They are never differences that affect major doctrines.

"Grace and peace" (v. 2)—The usual Greek salutation meant "greetings" or "favor from me to you." Yet Paul chose a different but related word, *charis,* "grace," in his salutation. Grace refers to God's unmerited favor bestowed on sinful individuals—with zero strings attached. And Paul appears to have used the best Greek translation available of a much-used Old Testament word used to refer to God's lovingkindness or mercy. Paul's greeting of "grace to you" or "God's unmerited favor be upon you" is more than a casual word of blessing. It's more like a prayer that the believers in Asia would continue to be filled with God's unearned, undeserved covenant love.

5. List some ways in which you have been a recipient of God's grace.

_____

_____

_____

In Paul's short introductory phrase that we might be tempted to overlook as mere formality, we find an entire sermon on unity. How so? After adding his own twist to turn the typical greeting into "grace," he also adds the Greek version of the Jewish *shalom:* peace. In combining "grace" from the standard Greek greeting and "peace" from the standard Hebrew greeting, he reminds his readers—both Gentile and Jewish readers—of the inclusiveness of the gospel. Notice he doesn't say, "Grace to the Gentiles, and peace to the Jews." Instead, he makes the two disparate groups the recipients of both grace and peace. Perhaps this is why Paul seems so fond of the greeting. The early church struggled with Jewish/Gentile divisions. Yet Paul's emphasis reminds his readers both in Ephesus and the present day that within the church there's no room for bigotry or "nation before gospel" thinking or snobbish class segregation. The Cross is the great equalizer.

WEDNESDAY: TO THE PRAISE OF HIS GLORY

1. Ephesians 1:3–23, our focus for the rest of the week. Circle every time Paul writes, "to the praise of his glory."

Ephesians 1:3 Blessed is the God and Father of our Lord Jesus Christ, who has blessed us with every spiritual blessing in the heavenly realms in Christ. **1:4** For he chose us in Christ before the foundation of the world that we may be holy and unblemished in his sight in love. **1:5** He did this by predestining us to adoption as his sons through Jesus Christ, according to the pleasure of his will—**1:6** to the praise of the glory of his grace that he has freely bestowed on us in his dearly loved Son. **1:7** In him we have redemption through his blood, the forgiveness of our trespasses, according to the riches of his grace **1:8** that he lavished on us in all wisdom and insight. **1:9** He did this when he revealed to us the secret of his will, according to his good pleasure that he set forth in Christ, **1:10** toward the administration of the fullness of the times, to head up all things in Christ—the things in heaven and the things on earth. **1:11** In Christ we too have been claimed as God's own possession, since we were predestined according to the one purpose of him who accomplishes all things according to the counsel of his will **1:12** so that we, who were the first to set our hope on Christ, would be to the praise of his glory. **1:13** And when you heard the word of truth (the gospel of your salvation)—when you believed in Christ—you were marked with the seal of the promised Holy Spirit, **1:14** who is the down payment of our inheritance, until the redemption of God's own possession, to the praise of his glory.

1:15 For this reason, because I have heard of your faith in the Lord Jesus and your love for all the saints, **1:16** I do not cease to give thanks for you when I remember you in my prayers. **1:17** I pray that the God of our Lord Jesus Christ, the Father of glory, may give you spiritual wisdom and revelation in your growing knowledge of him, **1:18**—since the eyes of your heart have been enlightened—so that you may know what is the hope of his calling, what is the wealth of his glorious inheritance in the saints, **1:19** and what is the incomparable greatness of his power toward us who believe, as displayed in the exercise of his immense strength. **1:20** This power he exercised in Christ when he raised him from the dead and seated him at his right hand in the heavenly realms **1:21** far above every rule and authority and power and dominion and every name that is named, not only in this age but also in the one to come. **1:22** And God put all things under Christ's feet, and he gave him to the church as head over all things. **1:23** Now the church is his body, the fullness of him who fills all in all.

2. Consider what this means: "Blessed is the God and Father of our Lord Jesus Christ, who has blessed us with every spiritual blessing in the heavenly realms in Christ" (v. 3). Often when we give thanks, we recall physical or relational blessings. But here we pause to consider that God has given his children *"every spiritual blessing in the heavenly realms in Christ."* Not a few blessings. But every blessing. The list is astonishing. If we were to make a list of the most fantastic things that could happen to us, it would not exceed this one. What has God blessed us with? Access to spiritual wisdom and revelation in our growing knowledge of him? Check. An inheritance as co-heir

with Christ himself? Check. Access to the resurrected Christ seated at the Father's right hand in this age and the one to come? Check. Redemption for and forgiveness of sins? Check. Status as God's chosen ones that we may be holy and unblemished in His sight in love? Check. Predestined to adoption into His family? Check. The objects of grace freely bestowed in his dearly loved Son? Check. Redemption through Christ's blood for the forgiveness of all trespasses? Check. Declared God's own possession? Check. God Himself in the person of the Holy Spirit living in us to empower us, comfort us, and help us become loving like Him? Check.

1. Ever wonder why God has placed humans on the planet? This passage helps answer the question, *Why am I here?* or *What is my purpose?* What does Paul's repetition of the phrase "to the praise of his glory" suggest is the ultimate end or purpose for which God has placed you and all humans on earth?

---

2. Go back to Monday of this week, where you underlined all the things God has done for those who have believed. Read each one. Let them whisper to you who you really are. The Book of Ephesians outlines your truest identity if you are a believer in Christ.

3. Think of additional blessings God has given you that have nurtured you in your spiritual life. List some of them here:

---

4. Examine your life. Ask the Spirit to show you areas where your thoughts and actions (whether things you have done or failed to do) keep Him from receiving the praise and glory He deserves.

_____

_____

_____

5. Write a short hymn, poem, or prayer of thanksgiving for the spiritual blessings God has lavished on you and for the life-changing work of the Spirit in you. Consider loading an MP3 player with songs of thanksgiving.

_____

_____

_____

_____

6. Go through Ephesians 1:1–14 and circle references to inheritance, adoption, and love.

> **Ephesians 1:1** From Paul, an apostle of Christ Jesus by the will of God, to the saints [in Ephesus], the faithful in Christ Jesus. **2** Grace and peace to you from God our Father and the Lord Jesus Christ!
>
> **1:3** Blessed is the God and Father of our Lord Jesus Christ, who has blessed us with every spiritual blessing in the heavenly realms in Christ. **1:4** For he chose us in Christ before the foundation of the world that we may be holy and unblemished in his sight in love. **1:5** He did this by predestining us to adoption as his sons through Jesus Christ, according to the pleasure of his will— **1:6** to the praise of the glory of his grace that he has freely bestowed on us in his dearly loved Son. **1:7** In him we have redemption through his blood, the forgiveness of our trespasses, according to the riches of his grace **1:8** that he lavished on us in all wisdom and insight. **1:9** He did this when he revealed to us the secret of his will, according to his good pleasure that he set forth in Christ, **1:10** toward the administration of the full-

ness of the times, to head up all things in Christ—the things in heaven and the things on earth. **1:11** In Christ we too have been claimed as God's own possession, since we were predestined according to the one purpose of him who accomplishes all things according to the counsel of his will **1:12** so that we, who were the first to set our hope on Christ, would be to the praise of his glory. **1:13** And when you heard the word of truth (the gospel of your salvation)—when you believed in Christ—you were marked with the seal of the promised Holy Spirit, **1:14** who is the down payment of our inheritance, until the redemption of God's own possession, to the praise of his glory.

We are God's own possession because He created us. But he also chose us for adoption into His family. Thus, we are his beloved treasures twice over. Consider what it means to be chosen:

"He chose us in Christ before the foundation of the world" (v. 4)—When our friends adopted a child from China, they sold t-shirts that said "Chosen" in large letters and "Ephesians 1:4" in small letters. Without thinking much about it, I wore mine on vacation. And later I realized from the way people looked at me (or was I imagining it?) that wearing a t-shirt that announced I was "chosen" could come off as arrogant. Certainly sometimes "chosen" is misunderstood to mean "exclusively superior." Yet in Paul's usage the word has quite the opposite sense. Lest we brag or feel smug about how brilliant we were to "choose" God or "accept Christ" (as if the Lord passed muster so we selected Him), the apostle reminds us that those who call on Christ for salvation (from our point of view) were actually chosen (from God's point of view) for divine mercy or favor. And His choice of us did not happen after we did something great. It happened long before we were born: Before the foundation of the world. There's mystery in the idea; in our finite minds humans cannot comprehend how we can choose only to find God chose first. But Paul's thrust is that being chosen should make us feel secure and thankful. If we did nothing to gain God's favor, we can also rest assured that nothing we do will cause us to lose it. Often, we ask, Why me? when trials come. Being elect should make us ask, Why me—that God should bestow such lavish kindness?

7. To what purpose did he choose us (v. 4), and how did he do it (v. 5)?

_____

_____

"Predestined" (v. 5, 11)—Some people read the word "predestined" and think humans have no choice, as if it doesn't matter what we do because God has decided it all anyway. We call such thinking "determinism," because it suggests all human actions are ultimately determined by causes external to our wills. How far this falls from the biblical teaching! The Greek word we translate as "predestined" does mean "to decide or appoint beforehand." And Paul uses it to describe what God decreed from eternity past. In each of the five times he uses the word throughout his epistles, he is talking about our redemption and growth in Christ, which ultimately brings glory to God. *Baker's Evangelical Dictionary* explains it this way: "God has a purpose that is determined long before it is brought to pass. God's purpose is one of love and grace (Deut. 7:6–8; Isa 41:8–9), above all because in love he predestined what should come to pass in his plan to save and to restore sinful humanity through Christ (Eph. 1:5)." And the point is this: as with election, far from patting ourselves on the back at our good fortune for "making it" into God's exclusive club, we should have the opposite response: humility and deep gratitude that we had nothing to do with it. Predestination means we bring nothing to the table that makes us worthy for God to accept us (2:8–9). And since we did nothing to make ourselves predestined, we can rest secure in our salvation. If we did nothing to earn God's favor, neither do we work to maintain his affection toward us. What security that gives us!

"According to the riches of his grace" (v. 8) – How rich is God's grace? It's infinite. And that is the degree to which we have received forgiveness for our sins. Do you ever feel you've sinned so much that God cannot possibly forgive you? Or perhaps you have a loved one who feels this way. Ephesians 1:8 teaches that God's forgiveness is meted out according to the infinite riches of his grace.

8. Write a prayer or poem of thanks to our all-knowing God for His infinite grace lavished on us in Christ.

_____

_____

_____

Not only did God predestine His children, but He ⌐
and gave us an inheritance to the praise of His glory (v. 5, 14).

Now, often there's a big gap between what we mean in Western
cultures today when we talk about adoption and what the biblical
writers meant. In the patriarchal cultures in which both Old and New
Testaments were set, the whole point of adoption was not family
building, but inheritance. If a man had no male heir, he would seek
an adult male on whom to bestow all his possessions. All his worldly
goods went to this heir—who was clearly not a child. So, adoption was
not usually about a little boy or girl entering a new family and being
nurtured as if that child were the parents' own, even though there
was a "joining a family" element to the adoption. Adoption of a non-
adult happened only when a child was found abandoned or when the
parents died and a home had to be found. Usually people were raised
by relatives in such cases.

Seven or eight decades before Paul wrote Ephesians, Julius Caesar
made provision in his will that after he died, his heir through adoption would be his great-nephew, Gaius Octavius Thurinus. This nine-
teen-year-old is known to us as Octavian or Caesar Augustus. Julius
Caesar's legal pronouncement made Augustus his son and heir. And
everyone in the world of Paul and John, the two New Testament writers who write about adoption, would have known this. The emphasis
in adoption in their time was on rights and inheritance. While these
are secondary when Westerners welcome a child through adoption (as
our family welcomed our daughter), son-ship and inheritance were
primary in the New Testament writers' minds.

The "leaving all one's possessions to a male heir" concept is part
of why Paul talks about "adoption as sons" rather than the more gen-
der-friendly "adoption as children." Females were not chosen for adult
adoption in Paul's world, only males. Paul's use of the analogy is not
to say the Roman culture was right or inspired. Rather, Paul was taking a common practice and showing how all who believe are like sons
in a Roman adoption—we inherit God's wealth! And as if all these
benefits were not enough, there is much more. There's redemption,
which involves an exchange. And we definitely get the good end of
the deal. We give God our trespasses, and, in exchange, Christ gives
his life. He gets our sins; we get his forgiveness: "In him we have

emption through his blood, the **forgiveness** of our trespasses, .cording to the riches of his grace that he lavished on us in all wisdom and insight." (vv. 7–8).

1. Read Ephesians 1:9–23. As you read, notice again what the text says is the one purpose for which we were made. It bears repeating, because Paul repeated it!

> **Ephesians 1:9** He did this when he revealed to us the secret of his will, according to his good pleasure that he set forth in Christ, **1:10** toward the administration of the fullness of the times, to head up all things in Christ—the things in heaven and the things on earth. **1:11** In Christ we too have been claimed as God's own possession, since we were predestined according to the one purpose of him who accomplishes all things according to the counsel of his will **1:12** so that we, who were the first to set our hope on Christ, would be to the praise of his glory. **1:13** And when you heard the word of truth (the gospel of your salvation)—when you believed in Christ—you were marked with the seal of the promised Holy Spirit, **1:14** who is the down payment of our inheritance, until the redemption of God's own possession, to the praise of his glory. **1:15** For this reason, because I have heard of your faith in the Lord Jesus and your love for all the saints, **1:16** I do not cease to give thanks for you when I remember you in my prayers. **1:17** I pray that the God of our Lord Jesus Christ, the Father of glory, may give you spiritual wisdom and revelation in your growing knowledge of him, **1:18**—since the eyes of your heart have been enlightened—so that you may know what is the hope of his calling, what is the wealth of his glorious inheritance in the saints, **1:19** and what is the incomparable greatness of his power toward us who believe, as displayed in the exercise of his immense strength. **1:20** This power he exercised in Christ when he raised him from the dead and seated him at his right hand in the heavenly realms **1:21** far above every rule and authority and power and dominion and every name that is named, not only in this age but also in the one to come. **1:22** And God put all things under Christ's feet, and he gave him to the church as head over all things. **1:23** Now the church is his body, the fullness of him who fills all in all.

"He revealed to us the secret of his will" (v. 9)—The idea of "oneness" is a key term in Ephesians, even in what Paul has to say about God's secret. We think of a secret as something hidden. But when Paul talks of God's secret or mystery, He is talking about how God had plans that in the past He kept to himself, but in Christ He made them known. Many people in first-century Asia believed the way to spiritual vitality was to be part of some inner circle with secrets. In their system of religion, God was accessible only to a select few. But Paul says the opposite. What was previously unknown but finally revealed is God's plan "to unite all things in Christ—the things in heaven and the things on earth" (v.10). Our great future hope is the fulfillment of what we ask in the Lord's Prayer: "Thy will be done on earth as it is in heaven." One day all shall be well. The writer of the old hymn "This Is My Father's World" ends it this way:

This is my Father's world.
O let me ne'er forget
That though the wrong
Seems oft so strong,
God is the ruler yet.
This is my Father's world:
The battle is not done:
Jesus who died shall be satisfied,
And earth and Heav'n be one.

2. Make a list of things that weigh most heavily on your heart. Your health? Conflict among those you love? The world and its systems?

_____

_____

_____

3. Pray through these, casting them at the feet of Christ and knowing that one day God will restore earth and heaven to full "shalom."

4. All God has done for us is for one purpose (vv. 11–12). This is our purpose for living. Paul has addressed who we are (God's children with a future inheritance and a future hope). He also says what we are here for. All God has done for us in love is for this one purpose. How does Paul describe it in verses 11–12?

_____

5. What happens from God's perspective when someone believes (v. 13–14)?

_____

6. What is the end goal of the believer's inheritance (v. 14)?

_____

Do you wonder what Paul is actually talking about when he refers to "inheritance" twice in Ephesians 1:13–19:

> **Ephesians 1:13** And when you heard the word of truth (the gospel of your salvation)—when you believed in Christ—you were marked with the seal of the promised Holy Spirit, **1:14** who is the down payment of our **inheritance,** until the redemption of God's own possession, to the praise of his glory. **1:15** For this reason, because I have heard of your faith in the Lord Jesus and your love for all the saints, **1:16** I do not cease to give thanks for you when I remember you in my prayers. **1:17** I pray that the God of our Lord Jesus Christ, the Father of glory, may give you spiritual wisdom and revelation in your growing knowledge of him, **1:18**—since the eyes of your heart have been enlightened—so that you may know what is the hope of his calling, what is the wealth of his glorious **inheritance** in the saints, **1:19** and what is the incomparable greatness of his power toward us who believe, as displayed in the exercise of his immense strength.

Our inheritance is not yet here, but it's coming. This is why some describe our position in Christ as "the already but not yet." In Christ we have already received massive spiritual benefits like forgiveness of sin and the indwelling of the Holy Spirit. But we have so much more to look forward to! Think of the ways in which our world is broken. How is your heart broken by sin? How have jealousy and lust and bitterness crept in? How is your body broken, and how are the bodies of those you love broken? Cancer. Alzheimer's. Pneumonia. Migraines. Disability. And what about societal woes such as racism and sexism, war and conflict, competition and greed, family violence, stealing and swindling and lying and cheating and injustice? What about disregard for the environment? Although we have wonderful blessings in Christ now, so much in our world remains unrestored. Thus, Paul says in his letter to the church at Rome, "All creation groans" (Rom. 8:22).

But he goes on to say, "we ourselves also, who have the first fruits of the Spirit, groan inwardly as we eagerly await our adoption, the redemption of our bodies. For in hope we were saved. Now hope that is seen is not hope, because who hopes for what he sees? "But if we hope for what we do not see, we eagerly wait for it with endurance" (Rom. 8:23–25).

Earth and heaven will be one. God will restore shalom. The dead will be raised; the blind will see; the lame will walk; the body ravaged by cancer will dance again. Believers who are estranged will be one as all who worship Christ will stand united in worship—people from every tribe and nation and tongue (Rev. 7:9). To the praise of His glory!

> *Man's chief and highest end is to glorify God, and fully to enjoy Him forever.*
> *—The Westminster Shorter Catechism, 1646*

Before pondering what this all means and how to apply it, we need to notice some important details in this passage:

7. How does Paul describe God the Father (v. 17)?

_____

8. What two things does Paul pray God will give readers (v. 17)?

_____

_____

We just noted how Paul described God the Father (Eph. 1:17). He wrote, "I pray that the God of our Lord Jesus Christ, the Father of glory, may give you spiritual wisdom . . . ."

We find the phrase "Father of glory" in the words of an old hymn, "Immortal, Invisible, God Only Wise" penned by Scottish minister Walter Chalmers Smith (1824–1908). (Consider loading it into your MP3 player.) The song contains this stanza:

> *Great Father of Glory, pure Father of Light*
> *Thine angels adore Thee, all veiling their sight;*
> *All praise we would render, O help us to see:*
> *'Tis only the splendor of light hideth Thee.*

Decades ago, C. S. Lewis ascended the pulpit of a church in Oxford and delivered a now-famous sermon, "The Weight of Glory." I highly recommend that you read it. But in the meantime, let's think about what Paul meant when he described glory—and why Lewis chose the word "weight" as part of his sermon title.

While we might think of glory as being nearly weightless like light, one word for "glory" in the Hebrew of the Old Testament, *kabod*, has a primitive root meaning the exact opposite: "weight" or "heaviness." So, the two words, weight and glory, have a connection. And while we often use "heavy" or "weighty" to describe negative things such as our burdens or bad news, think about how we might describe the gold in Fort Knox or a treasure chest. The heavier the weight, the greater the worth, right? Paul imagines the glory of the Father has having immeasurable weight because the Father has immeasurable worth. Elsewhere Paul wrote that "our present sufferings are not worth comparing to the glory that will be revealed in us" (Rom. 8:18). And Lewis combines the concepts of glory and weightiness in his book, *The Great Divorce*. There he observes, "All loneliness, angers, hatreds, envies, and itchings that [Hell] contains, if rolled into one single experience and put into the scale against the least moment of the joy that is felt by the least in Heaven, would have no weight that could be registered at all."

9. Write a short prayer, psalm, or hymn about the the Father's glory:

_____

_____

_____

10. Consider how your thoughts, actions, stillness, repentance, attitudes, and reconciliations could bring more glory to God. Jot some of your thoughts here.

_____

_____

_____

One key way Paul stresses that we glorify God is in *unity*. That unity includes our love for God and others with an ultimate end that earth and heaven would be one. Back in Ephesians 1:10 we read that the Father will "…head up [unite] all things in Christ, the things in heaven and the things on earth."

The translation here of "unite" as "head up" is rather unfortunate, as "head up" has the sense of leading without necessarily meaning unifying. To "head up" a committee usually means to preside over it. And while Jesus certainly presides over heaven and earth, that is not the idea Paul is stressing here. The Greek word translated here as "head up" is a word that the English Standard Version (ESV) and others render as unite. It was used of gathering things together and presenting them as a whole, like adding up a column of individual figures and putting the sum total at the top. The word was also used in rhetoric for summing up an address at the end, showing the relation of each part to the complete argument. In Romans 13:9 the word is used for the summing up of the commandments to the one essential: love.

Three ideas are present in the word here—restoration, unity, and oneness. Through sin, endless disorder and disintegration have come into the world; but, in the end, all things will be restored to their intended function and to their unity through being brought back to the obedience of Christ (cf. Col. 1:20).[13]

The concepts of oneness and unity—whether with Christ, with other believers, or in marriage—appear constantly throughout the Book of Ephesians. Read this sampling of examples:

> **Eph. 1:11** "according to the one purpose of him who accomplishes all things …"
>
> **Eph. 2:5** "alive together with Christ …"
>
> **Eph. 2:14** "the one who made both groups into one …"
>
> **Eph. 2:15** "He did this to create in himself one new man [church] out of two [Jew and Gentile], thus making peace …"
>
> **Eph. 2:16** "and to reconcile them both in one body to God through the cross …"
>
> **Eph. 2:18** "through him we both [Jew and Gentile] have access in one Spirit to the Father."

---

13 Francis Foulkes, *Ephesians: An Introduction and Commentary*, vol. 10, Tyndale New Testament Commentaries (Downers Grove, IL: Inter-Varsity Press, 1989), 61.

Eph. 2:19 "but you are fellow citizens with the saints . . ."

Eph. 2:21 "being joined together, grows into a holy temple in the Lord . . ."

Eph. 3:6 "through the gospel the Gentiles are fellow heirs, fellow members of the body, and fellow partakers of the promise in Christ Jesus."

Eph. 4:2 "bearing with one another in love..."

Eph. 4:3 "making every effort to keep the unity of the Spirit in the bond of peace."

Eph. 4:4 "There is one body and one Spirit, just as you too were called to the one hope of your calling."

Eph. 4:5 "one Lord, one faith, one baptism . . ."

Eph. 4:6 "one God and Father of all, who is over all and through all and in all."

Eph 4:13 "until we all attain to the unity of the faith . . ."

Eph. 4:16 "From him the whole body grows, fitted and held together through every supporting ligament. As each one does its part, the body grows in love.

Eph. 4:25 "for we are members of one another."

Eph. 4:32 "be kind to one another, compassionate, forgiving one another . . ."

Eph. 5:19 "speaking to one another in psalms . . ."

Eph. 5:21 "submitting to one another out of reverence to Christ."

Eph. 5:31 "the two will become one flesh."

Eph. 6:9 "you and they have the same master in heaven . . ."

It's quite a list, isn't it? All those references in six short chapters. Do you see from all this emphasis how important the unity (not to be confused with uniformity) of believers is to God?

11. What are some ways lack of unity among Christians damages the reputation of God?

_____

_____

12. What are some ways Christians showing love and service and grace bring glory to God?

_____

_____

_____

FRIDAY: HEAD OVER ALL

1. Pray for wisdom and read Ephesians 1:17–23.

> **Ephesians 1:17** I pray that the God of our Lord Jesus Christ, the Father of glory, may give you spiritual wisdom and revelation in your growing knowledge of him, **1:18**—since the eyes of your heart have been enlightened—so that you may know what is the hope of his calling, what is the wealth of his glorious inheritance in the saints, **1:19** and what is the incomparable greatness of his power toward us who believe, as displayed in the exercise of his immense strength. **1:20** This power he exercised in Christ when he raised him from the dead and seated him at his right hand in the heavenly realms **1:21** far above every rule and authority and power and dominion and every name that is named, not only in this age but also in the one to come. **1:22** And God put all things under Christ's feet, and he gave him to the church as head over all things. **1:23** Now the church is his body, the fullness of him who fills all in all.

2. What two things does Paul want his readers to know (vv. 18–19)?

_____

_____

3. Circle references to "strength" and "power" in verses 19–21. What sort of power has God demonstrated that no human possesses?

_____

_____

4. How can that power give hope to those who love God?

_____

_____

5. What two things did God do with Christ after raising Him from the dead (vv. 20–22)? (Notice the use of "far.")

_____

_____

6. What things now and in the age to come fall under the rule of Christ (vv. 21–22)?

_____

_____

_____

Pray through vv. 17–19 asking for yourself, your family, and the believers in your life the things Paul prayed for the Ephesians.

"Seated him at his right hand in the heavenly realms" (v. 20)—In English, if someone describes another person as "my right-hand man," it means a trusted assistant. But that is *not* what Paul means when he describes Jesus as seated at the right hand of the Father. In cultures in which the Bible was written, a high-ranking person who put someone "on his right hand" gave that person *equal* honor, authority, and dignity.

7. What gift did the Father give to the church (v. 22)?

_____

8. Go back and circle references in verses 18–23 to the words "head," "body," and "all."

9. When Paul calls Christ "head" in this passage, speaking of His authority or preeminence, what preposition does he use (v. 22)?

Circle one: Head of   Head over

Jesus is both "head over" all and "head of" His body the church. Paul states "head over" outright in this passage. And he says "body" to foreshadow what's coming—head of the body. Further exploration of the "head of the body" concept will come later.

10. Over what is Christ said to be lord (v. 21–22)?

_____

_____

_____

11. What areas of your life do you need to yield to the sovereign reign and rule of Christ?

_____

_____

12. Paul envisions a body in which Christ is the head and the collective church is His body; and Christ is Lord over all. With that picture in mind, what do you think it means that the church is the fullness of Christ (v. 23)?

_____

_____

13. List some ways in which you have seen or experienced the church, God's people, being the physical manifestation of Christ.

_____

_____

_____

_____

The church is the body, but not the place
Culture influences the church: One of the challenges of contemporary English language is that we generally use the word "church" interchangeably to refer to both the people of God and a physical building where they gather. But to New Testament writers, the church was only the people; their gathering places were in homes or public halls or under trees.

Church influences culture: Because of Paul's description of the church as Christ's body (v. 23), today people often (rightly) use the phrase "the body of Christ" as a synonym for "the church." But people became so accustomed to referring to the gathered church as "the body" that often many began to refer to any assembly (e.g., delegates) as a "body."

14. Ask the Spirit to help you consider how you can "be Christ" in your world. **Who** needs you to be the hands and feet and tear ducts of Jesus? **How** can you minister to those in need, whether to those you know or those you don't?

_____

_____

_____

_____

_____

Scripture: "[The Holy Spirit] is the down payment of our inheritance, until the redemption of God's own possession, to the praise of His glory" (Eph. 1:14).

My friend who was raised going to church every Sunday told me recently, "I just learned that the heaven believers will inhabit won't be somewhere up in the sky, but on earth—a new earth (see Rev. 21). How is it that after all these years I'm just now learning this?" Sadly, her experience is not that unusual. Often in teaching about heaven, we've missed God's good plan for restoring creation and how that plan intersects with our futures as his children.

In His Sermon on the Mount, Jesus said "The meek shall inherit the earth" (Matt. 5:5). Think about what the righteous will inherit: *the earth.* That would not be much of an inheritance if God planned to obliterate it. In fact, it tells us God has a good plan for this planet that does not involve its total annihilation.

In Ephesians 1, Paul seems to have in mind the same future that Jesus promised to the meek. The heirs of God possess the current spiritual blessings as a down payment; in the future, the literal physical earth in a full restored state will be theirs too. The plan of God is to unite heaven and earth, not to scrap this planet in favor of a sky-only abode. Think of the most beautiful place on earth and imagine the whole of creation at that level of restoration. And you living there. In a world in which most religions and philosophies elevate the spiritual over the physical, our Lord actually gave physicality its ultimate dig-nifier: He enrobed himself in it. Jesus's incarnation or "enfleshment" makes it clear that matter is not evil. God created matter! And Jesus's bodily death, resurrection, and ascension—these all dignify it. Jesus did not die an ethereal death, rise from the grave in an ethereal body, or ascend to heaven in an ethereal state. The God in whom all matter was created clothed Himself in this creation.

Some of the best lines in our Christmas carols express this reality:

Veiled in flesh the Godhead see, Hail the incarnate Deity...
Lo, He abhors not the Virgin's womb...
Word of the Father, now in flesh appearing...
O come to us, abide with us, our Lord—Immanuel [God with us]

Flesh. Blood. Incarnation. Bodily resurrection. God made and embraces matter. While humans have corrupted it and sin has ravaged it, God's plan is to restore it. (This is why for many centuries Christians have tended to choose burial over cremation. The corpse serves as a symbolic reminder that God will re-enflesh the body of his child.)

While Paul begins Ephesians 1 with a description of all the spiritual blessings we have in Christ, he ends his chapter with a look at the world to come in which the spiritual and the physical will be united and restored, and all shall be well.

In the meantime, God's people filled with the Spirit are the physical manifestation of the invisible Christ: "The church is his body the fulness of him who fills all in all" (v. 23). Whom can you serve today as a manifestation of the presence of Christ in the power of the Spirit?

For Memorization: "Blessed is the God and Father of our Lord Jesus Christ, who has blessed us with every spiritual blessing in the heavenly realms in Christ" (Eph. 1:3).

Prayer: *Father God, thank you for the blessings you have lavished upon your children in Christ. Thank you for choosing and predestining and forgiving and restoring. Please grant me the Spirit of wisdom and revelation to know you better. Open my eyes that I might know the hope to which You have called me. Help me to more fully comprehend the riches of the glorious inheritance You have promised. Grant me the strength through the Spirit to live in hope, knowing a glorious inheritance awaits me. Help me to live a life that brings unity to your people and glory to Your name through Christ our Lord, Amen.*

WEEK 2 OF 6

Reconciled: Ephesians 2

SUNDAY: BETTER-THAN-FIJI GRACE

Scripture: For by grace you are saved through faith, and this is not from your-selves, it is the gift of God; it is not from works, so that no one can boast. For we are his workmanship, having been created in Christ Jesus for good works that God prepared beforehand so we may do them (Eph. 2:8–10).

During the time of year when retailers exchange their orange pumpkins for ornament-filed trees, our minds drift to gifts. After checking our lists twice, most of us give presents to loved ones regard-less of their naughty-or-nice status. And our Christmas-giving systems often rely on reciprocation, not grace.

Have your neighbors ever dropped off a basket of jams while you fumbled empty handed? Most of us in such a situation would run out to buy them an equivalent Hickory Farms cheese box. Imagine the hor-ror if your brother unwrapped a mug you bought him as you opened a gift certificate from him for an all-expenses-paid trip to Fiji. If we're honest, we have a hard time receiving something we don't deserve, especially if we cannot reciprocate. And yet, that is grace—getting something we cannot take any credit for. That is why Paul adds to his explanation of such grace "that no one should boast" (Eph. 2:9).

Why would God do all that? Paul answers, "For you are his workmanship" (v. 10). That word translated "workmanship" refers to a masterpiece of art, and it is attributed to God alone at creation. God made us. He designed us. We had nothing to do with our own creation. When we create, whether it be a skyscraper, scrapbook page, or prose, we start with vision, work with diligence, and pay attention to the details. God did and does the same with His human creations. He intentionally produced each of us. And to what purpose? "For good works that God prepared beforehand so we may do them" (v. 10).

Sometimes we get the order backwards. We may do good works thinking these will earn us salvation or favor with God. But when sin ruled us, in His grace God saved us—not due to anything we had done. Once we have received His grace, our response of good works flows from love and worship and gratitude, not to earn salvation! God already prepared the way, and we get to walk in it. God delights in us, and he created us to be like Him—giving water to the thirsty, bread to the hungry, and clothing to the naked. In doing so, we thrive as we fulfill God's purpose for us.

Have you received his grace? Thank God that Christ died for you, through nothing you have done. Are you continuing to walk in grace, motivated by gratitude rather than thinking you can earn points with God?

Are you living in line with God's purpose for you, his marvelous creation—showing that same love and better-than-a-trip-to-Fiji grace to others?

"Praise be to the God and Father of our Lord Jesus Christ!" (1:3).

MONDAY: BEFORE AND AFTER PHOTOS

1. Pray, asking the Spirit for insight. Then read Ephesians 2.

Ephesians 2:1 And although you were dead in your transgressions and sins, **2:2** in which you formerly lived according to this world's present path, according to the ruler of the kingdom of the air, the ruler of the spirit that is now energizing the sons of disobedience, **2:3** among whom all of us also formerly lived out our lives in the cravings of our flesh, indulging the desires of the flesh and the mind, and were by nature children of wrath even as the rest...

2:4 But God, being rich in mercy, because of his great love with which he loved us, **2:5** even though we were dead in transgressions, made us alive together with Christ—by grace you are saved!—**2:6** and he raised us up with him and seated us with him in the heavenly realms in Christ Jesus, **2:7** to demonstrate in the coming ages the surpassing wealth of his grace in kindness toward us in Christ Jesus. **2:8** For by grace you are saved through faith, and this is not from yourselves, it is the gift of God; **2:9** it is not from works, so that no one can boast. **2:10** For we are his workmanship, having been created in Christ Jesus for good works that God prepared beforehand so we may do them.

2:11 Therefore remember that formerly you, the Gentiles in the flesh—who are called "uncircumcision" by the so-called "circumcision" that is performed on the body by human hands—**2:12** that you were at that time without the Messiah, alienated from the citizenship of Israel and strangers to the covenants of promise, having no hope and without God in the world. **2:13** But now in Christ Jesus you who used to be far away have been brought near by the blood of Christ. **2:14** For he is our peace, the one who made both groups into one and who destroyed the middle wall of partition, the hostility, **2:15** when he nullified in his flesh the law of commandments in decrees. He did this to create in himself one new man out of two, thus making peace, **2:16** and to reconcile them both in one body to God through the cross, by which the hostility has been killed. **2:17** And he came and preached peace to you who were far off and peace to those who were near, **2:18** so that through him we both have access in one Spirit to the Father. **2:19** So then you are no longer foreigners and noncitizens, but you are fellow citizens with the saints and members of God's household, **2:20** because you have been built on the foundation of the apostles and prophets, with Christ Jesus himself as the cornerstone. **2:21** In him the whole building, being joined together, grows into a holy temple in the Lord, **2:22** in whom you also are being built together into a dwelling place of God in the Spirit.

2. Circle the big transition marker in this passage: "But God" (v. 4).

3. What is Paul's general assessment of all humans before he says, "but God" (vv. 1–3).

4. Go through today's passage and fill in the two columns below to get a picture of humanity versus God's grace. On the left put the evidence of all humanity's broken state; on the right, list what Paul says God has done about it.

Humanity in our broken state	What God has done

Tuesday: The Bad News Before the Good News

1. Read below the passage for the day, Ephesians 2:1–3. Let's look more specifically at how the apostle Paul describes the state of all people before God reconciles them to himself (vv. 1–3).

> **Ephesians 2:1-3:** And although you were dead in your transgressions and sins, in which you formerly lived according to this world's present path, according to the ruler of the kingdom of the air, the ruler of the spirit that is now energizing the sons of disobedience, among whom all of us also formerly lived out our lives in the cravings of our flesh, indulging the desires of the flesh and the mind, and were by nature children of wrath even as the rest . . .

2. Paul says that those without Christ live according to the ruler who opposes God. What two descriptors does he use for this ruler (v. 2)?

"Dead in your trespasses and sins" (v. 1)—"Sin" is not just individual sins we commit. It is a realm that has rendered humans spiritually lifeless. We commit sins because we inhabit the realm of sin.

When people die physically, we know they have no breath or movement in them; death leaves them powerless. Dead people cannot awaken or improve their condition. Likewise, sin as a ruler separates us from God and leaves us powerless to repair the damage. We have no spiritual breath; we have no capacity to heal from the effects of sin. We must depend on God to conquer sin and raise us to life.

Does Paul repeat himself when he refers both to "transgressions" and "sins" (Eph. 2:1)? Yes and no. In this verse, scholars translate the Greek word *paraptōma* as "transgression" and *hamartia* as "sin." *Paraptōma* is used twenty-three times in the New Testament, and can be translated as trespass, sin, offense, or transgression. It means to fall down, deviate from the truth, or make a false step. Our English dictionaries define it as violating a law or command. *Hamartia* is used 174 times in the New Testament, and translators almost always render it as "sin." It means to fail, to miss the mark (as in archery), to commit an evil deed, to violate God's divine law. Interestingly, in our English dictionaries the definition of sin varies from offending a religious law to wasting any substance, like food. In Greek, *hamartia* carries heavier weight, but in modern English, "transgression" gets our attention. We don't call eating too much chocolate cake a transgression, but we may joke that it's a sin to throw away our leftover pot roast or describe rich desserts as sinful. Paul used both words, although varying in root meaning, to convey an essential point. We fell down when we gossiped. We violated God's law when we lied in that report to our boss. We missed the mark when we drank too much wine the other night. Despite our modern usage of the words "sin" and "transgression," together they still drive the point home: we need Jesus.

"Ruler of the kingdom of the air" (v. 2)—In the past, some used this verse to argue against Christian radio stations, because such people thought it taught that Satan ruled the airways. That is not Paul's point! According to Jewish tradition, demons lived and exerted their power in the air, the realm surrounding humans.[14] Most theologians think Paul is referring here to the accuser. The writers of the four Gospels (Matthew, Mark, Luke and John) also use the word archōn (translated here as "ruler") to refer to Satan's reign.

Although Paul has in mind both males and females, he describes the before-Christ identity of each person as "sons of disobedience" (v. 1).

"Sons of disobedience" (v. 2)—The word for "sons" here, *huios,* can strictly mean male offspring. But it is also used more broadly to connote descendants in general. So, some translations use "those who" instead of "sons," seeking to express the intended meaning rather than translating in a way that loses meaning but keeps rigid wording. The phrases "sons of disobedience" (vs. 2) and "children of

14. Vincent, M. R. (1887). *Word Studies in the New Testament.* (Vol. 3, p. 374). New York: Charles Scribner's Sons.

wrath" (vs. 3) mean the same thing.[15] The stress is on "disobedience." Thus, we can read the phrase as "people who disobey God" or "those who rebel." [16] That is, we act just like our parent, disobedience.

3. Whom does Paul include under that description of "sons of disobedience" (v. 2).

_____

4. According to Paul, what was the source of humans' cravings, and what did humans indulge (v. 3)?

_____

5. What are some ways the mind not set on the Spirit indulges the flesh and the mind?

_____

_____

_____

"By nature children of wrath" (v. 3)—Often we think of the wrath of God as an out-of-control emotion, as we envision someone with unbridled fury. Thus, the "wrath of God" may seem out of character when attributed to One who is otherwise described as loving and long-suffering. But as theologian Fleming Rutledge explains, "[God's wrath] is not an *emotion*; it is God's righteous activity in setting right what is wrong."[17] God's wrath is His justice in motion.

6. All these descriptions of the without-Christ person support the idea that, apart from Christ, every single person stands in need of grace. Have you received the grace of God? If so, give thanks. If not, what is holding you back?

_____

15. J. Armitage Robinson, *Commentary on Ephesians,* (Grand Rapids: Kregel Publications, 1979), 49.
16. Glenn H. Graham, *An Exegetical Summary of Ephesians,* (Dallas: SIL International, 1997), 110–1.
17. Rutledge, Fleming. *The Crucifixion: Understanding the Death of Jesus Christ.* (Grand Rapids, Michigan: William B. Eerdman's Publishing Company, 2015), p. 132.

History and English teachers are said to have compiled student bloopers on World History papers that author Richard Lederer collected and published. In one such blooper, the student confused "circumscribed" and "circumcised," with unfortunate results. The offending paper said, "Sir Francis Drake circumcised the world with a 100-foot clipper." Yikes!

Long before the descendants of Abraham multiplied into a nation, God told his covenant people to engage in a practice that set them apart: circumcision. So what exactly is it?

"Circumcision" (v. 11)—the cutting off of the foreskin of a penis on a young boy or man, but especially a baby as a religious rite. (Female circumcision is now called "female genital mutilation" [FGM] and is actually not an equivalent practice, even though it was called "circumcision.") God gave the command to Abraham and his descendants to circumcise their sons: "For the generations to come every male among you who is eight days old must be circumcised, including those born in your household or bought with money from a foreigner—those who are not your offspring" (Gen. 17:12). Circumcision, this sign of God's covenant, was done to male bodies on their most personal part to remind them of the special relationship they had as God's own people. (The Christian equivalent that designates a person as being in covenant with God is baptism.)

1. With this in mind, pray for insight and read Ephesians 2:11–12:

> **Ephesians 2:11** Therefore remember that formerly you, the Gentiles in the flesh—who are called "uncircumcision" by the so-called "circumcision" that is performed on the body by human hands—that you were at that time without the Messiah, alienated from the citizenship of Israel and strangers to the covenants of promise, having no hope and without God in the world.

In the previous section of Ephesians, Paul has just established that every human is dead in sin but has been shown grace. Having argued that all stand in need of the Savior, Paul challenges his primarily Gentile audience to consider something: just how much their non-Jewish pedigree added to their "outsider" status. He paints a very dark picture so both Jew and Gentile will grasp the greatness of God's grace.

2. What is the lone imperative (command) in these two verses (v. 11–12)?

"Gentiles in the flesh" (v. 11)—Often when Paul speaks of "the flesh," he is talking about being ruled by one's cravings. Yet here he also means the phrase more literally. That is, in the physical body. Most of those reading his letter were physically "Gentiles in the flesh." They lacked the bodily "marker" that identified them as children of Abraham; instead, they were "children of wrath even as the rest . . . " (v. 3). Not only did they lack the genealogy that gave them the inherited blessings of Abraham, but they also lacked the sign on their physical bodies (circumcision) that identified them as recipients of God's promises. Thus, all—both Jew and Gentile—were lost ("even as the rest"). The Gentiles were just lost as outsiders. The phrase translated here as "Gentiles in the flesh" was an unflattering Jewish idiom that meant "nations in the flesh." But Paul doesn't let his own people off the hook here. He describes them as the "so-called circumcision." Why? Both groups lacked "circumcision of the heart."

"By human hands" (v. 12)—When Paul refers to things as "made by human hands," he usually has something negative in mind. Like idols. Certainly, he thinks made-by-hand things are inferior to anything God makes. So, Paul is subtly setting up his readers for something better when he describes even circumcision as being "made by human hands."

This "made by human hands" emphasis shows up repeatedly in Paul's thinking. Bear in mind, he had a fantastic pedigree as a Jew. He told his friends at Philippi that he was "circumcised on the eighth day, of the people of Israel, of the tribe of Benjamin, a Hebrew of Hebrews; as to the law, a Pharisee; as to zeal, a persecutor of the church; as to righteousness under the law, blameless" (Phil. 3:5–7). Thus, he is not addressing everyone's inferior circumcision as an outsider, but as an insider.

When Paul preached to Gentiles in Athens, he looked around at the people's many altars to gods in the pantheon, and he said, "The God who made the world and everything in it is the Lord of heaven and earth and does not live in temples *built by hands*. And he is not served by human hands, as if he needed anything" (Acts 17:24–25, NIV).

Paul will go on to argue in our text here in Ephesians that something humans do (circumcise the body) is inferior to what God does (circumcise the heart). Although Gentiles were "left out" in earlier times over externals (circumcision), now through Christ they can enter fellowship. A ritual practice with an originally good intent cannot keep them out.

In his letter to the church at Colossae, Paul argues that physical circumcision means nothing spiritual, because God has circumcised the believing Gentiles with a better circumcision—that of the heart (Col. 2:11).

Paul explains this idea even more fully in his letter to the church at Rome (it is really important to him!): "For a person is not a Jew who is one outwardly, nor is circumcision something that is outward in the flesh, but someone is a Jew who is one inwardly, and circumcision is of the heart by the Spirit and not by the written code (Rom. 2:28–29).

Paul's seemingly radical thinking about "circumcision of the heart" here is actually not a new idea. It came from God Himself centuries earlier. Six-and-a-half centuries earlier, to be exact. As recorded by the prophet Jeremiah, God told his people that he preferred heart-righteousness to externals: "Circumcise yourselves to the LORD and remove the foreskins of your heart" (Jer. 4:4).

3. What four disadvantages did Gentiles have that had made them far away (v. 12)?

_____

_____

Alienated from the citizenship of Israel (v. 12)—Paul probably has in mind here not the Gentile's geographic location but their exclusion from the social/political/theological covenant community of Israel.

Strangers to the covenants of promise (v. 12)—Like refugees without rights in a new land, the Gentiles were outsiders when it came to the amazing covenants God made with the Jewish people.

Without God (v. 12)—The irony in Paul's basically calling Gentiles in their pre-Christ state "atheists" is that Gentiles in the first-century Greco-Roman world called Jews "atheists" for their refusal to worship the many gods in the pantheon.

So, there it is . . . Paul has told the Gentiles to remember how lost they were. But he gives little hints and reminders that the Jews were lost too. One group may have had more advantages, but they were all lost. Yet the next words in Paul's text will change everything: "But now in Christ Jesus . . ."

These are the pivot words. On them both horizontal and vertical relationships change: "But now in Christ Jesus you who used to be far away have been brought near by the blood of Christ" (v. 13).

If you are a Gentile, give thanks that through Christ the covenant blessings of the Jewish people are extended to you. If you are Jewish, give thanks that through your heritage and your long-promised Messiah, all nations of the world are blessed (see Gen. 22:18).

God's plan all along was inclusion. Abraham was chosen that his descendants might be the means of grace for all who were lost. External circumcision was intended to signify an internal commitment, but it led to insider/outsider status. The promised Jewish Messiah came for all the world—to reconcile all people to God and all humans to each other.

THURSDAY: THE EMBODIMENT OF PEACE

On Wednesday of this week, we saw how Jesus broke down the barriers that separated Gentiles from God. Paul will now turn his focus from the restoration of the vertical (God/human) relationship to the reconciliation of a horizontal one (Gentile/Jew). Through His body broken by hostility, Jesus unites two hostile groups, bringing "both groups into one" (2:14).

1. Pray, asking for wisdom and read the text for today, Ephesians 2:13–18:

> **Ephesians 2:13** But now in Christ Jesus you who used to be far away have been brought near by the blood of Christ. **2:14** For he is our peace, the one who made both groups into one and who destroyed the middle wall of partition, the hostility, **2:15** when he nullified in his flesh the law of commandments in decrees. He did this to create in himself one new man out of two, thus making peace, **2:16** and to reconcile them both in one body to God through the cross, by which the hostility has been killed. **2:17** And he came and preached peace to you who were far off and peace to those who were near, **2:18** so that through him we both have access in one Spirit to the Father.

Bear in mind that these verses still fall within the range of things Paul wants his readers to remember (v. 11).

1. What one thing "brings near" Jew and Gentile (v. 13)?

_____

2. Paul describes Christ as "our peace." According to Paul, what two things did Jesus do to bring about this peace (vv. 14)?

_____

"The middle wall of partition, the hostility" (v. 15)—What middle wall is Paul talking about? He's probably using a bit of double meaning here. He says outright that Jesus Christ destroyed the hostility or enmity between the two groups. There was a metaphorical wall of animosity. But Paul probably also knows that the idea of a "middle wall of partition" will resonate with his Jewish readers, as a literal wall physically divides Jew and Gentile in the Jewish temple in Jerusalem at this time. In Solomon's original temple, we have zero evidence that a physical barrier existed:

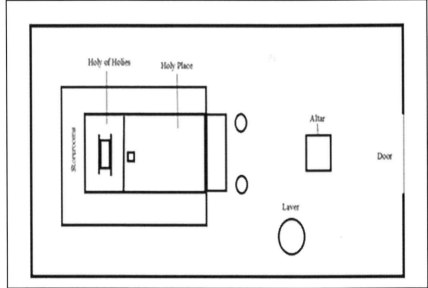

Solomon's Temple

Later Herod the Great erected the new or second temple (see below) that replaced (but was never recognized by God) the destroyed temple of Solomon. And when Herod did so, some overt ethnic and gender barriers appeared. These had not existed as part of the original temple. Apparently on command of the Jews, "the court of the Gentiles" was erected—Gentiles were prohibited from entering space where the Jews were. The Gentiles desiring to worship Yahweh (God's covenant name) stayed in the outer court; a middle wall kept them from going in. Paul is doubtless using this physical barrier as an illustration. When Jesus came, He shattered to pieces that separating wall and declared all welcome. That wall had caused ethnic hostility; Jesus abolished it.

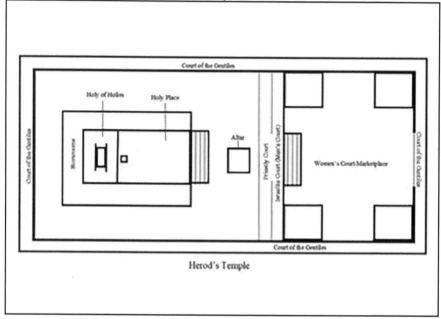

Herod's Temple

And not only did the blood of Christ abolish the physical wall and the hostility it both caused and represented. He also did something to the Jewish Law: "he nullified in his flesh (i.e., via his violent death) the law of commandments in decrees" (v. 15).

3. What two reasons does Paul give for Jesus' nullifying the Law (vv. 15–16)?

Often when we think of the Bible teaching about a "new man" or a "new person," we think of the new creation God makes of redeemed humans in Christ (2 Cor. 5:1). Yet, while that concept is true, that is not what Paul is talking about here. Paul loves to use the image of separate parts becoming one body. In Ephesians 5, he describes marriage as a head and a body—two becoming one. And here also, he describes Jew and Gentile as one new person, and not a person at war with himself, either. Paul did not say that Christ brought tolerance. Rather, Christ brought *shalom*.

4. List some groups of people who are estranged in your world.

_____

_____

5. My friend, a Hutu from Rwanda, married a Tutsi. Both are believers in Christ. Their marriage reveals the astonishing reconciliation that Christ can bring between people from groups who hate and murder each other. How have you seen Christ change lives to make enemies into unlikely friends?

_____

_____

Paul summarizes why Christ endured the hostility of humans to the point of death:

"He did this to create in himself one new man out of two, thus making peace, and to reconcile them both in one body to God through the cross, by which the hostility has been killed. And He came and preached peace to you who were far off [Gentiles] and peace to those who were near [Jews], so that through Him we both have access in one Spirit to the Father" (vv. 15–18).

When first-century Jewish Christians heard these words from Paul, they would have thought of statements the prophet Isaiah penned centuries earlier. As Isaiah prophesied of coming judgment and exile, he also offered hope of the Messiah. Isaiah told his listeners that Messiah would come as a messenger proclaiming peace, good news, and deliverance (Isa 52:7). Thus, when Paul says to the Ephesians that Jesus came to preach peace, he is asserting that Jesus Christ fulfilled Isaiah's prophecy.

But Isaiah offered more than words of warning and judgment. He also comforted the Jews. He insisted that those who were "far off" (i.e. in exile), as well as Jews who were "near" (i.e. in the land of Israel), would experience restoration (Isa 59:17).

In his letter to the mostly Gentile Ephesians, Paul uses these familiar prophetic words. But he broadens the ethnic audience. Instead of referring to the physical location of Jews as Isaiah did, Paul speaks of spiritual proximity. He argues that God offers peace to the Gentile (v. 17), even though the Gentile was distant from Him (vv.11–13). So again, Paul is arguing that the gospel is for everyone, Jew and Gentile alike. The shed blood of Jesus merges these two groups who once stood in violent opposition (vv. 14–17). Christ is the peace that draws people into unlikely unity. The Gentiles have gone from "stranger" status to that of beloved family members. In one Spirit both groups have access to the Father.

And there's something else important to note about the peace Jesus brought. When we talk about the peace of God, it does not necessarily mean calm circumstances or a feeling of serenity. These may depend on circumstances, which, as my friend Jennifer says, "are as changeable as the buzzing of a fly or the sting of a careless word." She goes on to say, "Peace for the believer is much more profound. In Christ, we have peace with God, though we in our 'fallen-ness' are corrupt beyond deserving any peace of any kind. God in his great mercy chose to send his Son for our salvation. And when He did this, he did it so that anyone who enters in by faith in Christ can have it. It isn't a feeling; it is a reality beyond any experience we expect to find through our performance or our surroundings. Do you long for peace? If you believe in Christ, you have it. He has already given it to you. If you want to experience it, walk in His guiding shadow, and make the simple choice to believe it. Simple? Yes. Easy? No. But faith believes in a reality we cannot always see, only to find that when we believe, what was shrouded in darkness becomes crystal clear."

6. What in your life leaves you feeling hopeless or conflicted? What would it look like to believe you have God's peace in that area?

---

7. Jesus changes lives. There is no reconciler like Jesus! There is no unifier of warring groups like the gospel of Christ. Whom do you know that needs Him?

_____

_____

_____

Pray for those you listed. Ask God to open hearts and use you to help them see the beauty of God.

Friday: Status Update

1.Pray for wisdom and read Paul's words summarizing the Gentiles' status update:

> **Ephesians 2:19-22:** So then you are no longer foreigners and noncitizens, but you are fellow citizens with the saints and members of God's household, because you have been built on the foundation of the apostles and prophets, with Christ Jesus himself as the cornerstone. In him the whole building, being joined together, grows into a holy temple in the Lord, in whom you also arc being built together into a dwelling place of God in the Spirit.

When Paul writes "so then," he has a "so what" coming. And what he is about to say is pretty amazing.

2. See the contrast in verse 19? Fill in the columns to see that contrast more visually:

What the Gentiles are no longer	What the Gentiles are now

"Fellow citizens" (v. 19)—Paul tells the Ephesians they are "fellow citizens" of God's household. In doing so, he tells Gentile believers that they have the same standing before God as Jewish ones. It was a pretty big deal in his day to unite the Jews and Gentiles, people who formerly hated and wanted nothing to do with each other. Also, the Jews thought they had exclusive access to God, so the idea of adding Gentiles to the fellowship of God's people would have stunned them. Additionally, unlike in the USA where everyone born in the country is automatically a citizen, only certain people (never slaves, for example) were citizens. What does all this mean for us today as citizens of nations such as the USA, England, or India? Jesus told believers to obey the law of the land (Mark 12:17), and Paul implored readers to submit to those in authority over them (Rom. 13:1). But the believer's primary citizenship, our first loyalty, is to God's kingdom. And just as in Christ the Jew and Gentile unite, so do Kenyans and Americans. Irish and Russians. Koreans and Ethiopians. Democrats and Republicans and Independents. As do those with black, brown, and white bodies.

Since the law of our land does not require us to sing the national anthem or pledge to the American flag when we gather in church, should we? We can and should thank God for the religious freedoms afforded us in the country in which we live. But we must always remember that as members of God's family, the church's primary and ultimate allegiance is to Christ and our fellow believers—far more than to fellow citizens in our country and its parties. As members of one another, we are to prioritize our kingdom citizenship and oneness over all other loyalties (e.g., ethnic, national, political, family).

3. The Gentiles' outsider status changed because someone preached the good news to them: "because you have been built on the foundation of the apostles and prophets, with Christ Jesus himself as the cornerstone" (v. 20). Paul seems to envision an unfinished, living, growing temple. To get the visual picture of what he has in view, notice Jesus's name in the chart on the opposite page in the position of chief cornerstone. Everything else is aligned against that stone. The twelve apostles comprise the foundation—with Paul added and Judas Iscariot replaced by Matthias. On the next layer you could add other sent-ones ("apostles") and prophets, including Phillip's unmarried daughters who prophesied (Acts 21:9), as well as Junia (Rom. 16:7). Above these write the names of people who have taught you the Bible. Write your own name on a stone above these. And in each square write the name of a brother or sister in Christ—dead or living, Jewish or Gentile.

Jesus, the Cornerstone						
Peter / Andrew						
John / Thomas						
Jude/ Judas, Judas not Iscariot)						
Philip / Bartholomew						
Matthew / Levi						
James the Less						
Simon the Zealot/ Matthias						
Paul						

In the chart pictured on the previous page, Christ is part of the very foundation. The chief cornerstone had to be perfect, because it served as a plumb line against which every other stone lined up. If the cornerstone was crooked, the building would lean and fall. By choosing this image, Paul draws on an Old Testament picture. The prophet Isaiah eight centuries earlier wrote, "This is what the sovereign master, the Lord, says: 'Look, I am laying a stone in Zion [Jerusalem], an approved stone, set in place as a precious cornerstone for the foundation.

> A number of Christian artists have recorded songs about Christ being the cornerstone. Consider finding some and loading them into devices you can play on the way to the grocery store or work.

The one who maintains his faith will not panic. I will make justice the measuring line, fairness the plumb line'" (Isa. 28:16–17). See the connection to the cornerstone and measuring/straightness? Interestingly, Matthew tells of Jesus in the temple courts talking with Jewish religious leaders. There Jesus quotes a psalm about the cornerstone in reference to himself: "Have you never read in the Scriptures: 'The stone the builders rejected has become the cornerstone'" (Matt. 21:42, citing Ps. 118:22). He would be rejected by the leaders, yet he would be the cornerstone to God's living temple, the church.

Paul clearly has the temple in mind as he speaks of uniting Jew and Gentile to create a spiritual temple. His description of the church as comprised of Jewish and Gentile "stones" stands in contrast to the image of the aforementioned dividing wall in the second temple. That stone structure was a four-foot-high marble wall that divided Jew and Gentile and was thus a source of insider/outsider hostility. First-century historian Josephus in *The Wars of the* Jews described it: "On it [the wall] stood pillars at equal distances from one another, declaring the law of purity, some in Greek and some in Roman letters that no foreigner should go within the sanctuary . . . under pain of death" (5.5.2).

Paul knew this barrier well. In fact, many believe he was writing what we know as the Book of Ephesians from a Roman prison precisely because of that wall in Jerusalem ("For this reason I, Paul, the prisoner of Christ Jesus for the sake of you Gentiles..." 3:1). Here is how the writer of Acts, probably Luke, describes the events that transpired. (As you're reading, notice the mention of Asia—where Ephesus is located—and what city Paul's Gentile companion in the story was from.)

After we arrived in Jerusalem, the brethren received us gladly. And the following day Paul went in with us to James, and all the elders were present. After he had greeted them, he began to relate one by one the things which God had done among the Gentiles through his ministry. And when they heard it they began glorifying God; and they said to him, "You see, brother, how many thousands there are among the Jews of those who have believed, and they are all zealous for the Law; and they have been told about you, that you are teaching all the Jews who are among the Gentiles to forsake Moses, telling them not to circumcise their children nor to walk according to the customs. What, then, is to be done? They will certainly hear that you have come. Therefore do this that we tell you. We have four men who are under a vow; take them and purify yourself along with them, and pay their expenses so that they may shave their heads; and all will know that there is nothing to the things which they have been told about you, but that you yourself also walk orderly, keeping the Law. But concerning the Gentiles who have believed, we wrote, having decided that they should abstain from meat sacrificed to idols and from blood and from what is strangled and from fornication." Then Paul took the men, and the next day, purifying himself along with them, went into the temple giving notice of the completion of the days of purification, until the sacrifice was offered for each one of them.

When the seven days were almost over, the Jews from Asia, upon seeing him in the temple, began to stir up all the crowd and laid hands on him, crying out, "Men of Israel, come to our aid! This is the man who preaches to all men everywhere against our people and the Law and this place; and besides *he has even brought Greeks into the temple and has defiled this holy place."* For they had previously seen Trophimus the Ephesian in the city with him, and they supposed that Paul had brought him into the temple. Then all the city was provoked, and the people rushed together, and taking hold of Paul they dragged him out of the temple, and immediately the doors were shut. While they were seeking to kill him, a report came up to the commander of the Roman cohort that all Jerusalem was in confusion. At once he took along some soldiers and centurions and ran down to them; and when they saw the commander and the soldiers, they stopped beating Paul. Then the commander came up and took hold of him, and ordered him to be bound with two chains; and he began asking who he was and what he had done (Acts 21:17–33, italics added).

Paul was arrested for a crime he did not commit due to the animosity Jews had for Gentiles and the misguided concern that Paul was "polluting" the temple by disrespecting the wall. It was this very accusation he was trying to avoid by being there! In contrast, Paul argues in his letter that in Christ the Father is constructing a new temple *not made with hands*: "In him [Christ] the whole building, being joined together, grows into a holy temple in the Lord, in whom you also are being built together into a dwelling place of God in the Spirit (Eph. 2:21–22). In this scenario, Jew and Gentile are no longer at odds with each other, but are one.

Have you ever heard someone say your church building is God's temple or the house of the Lord? Maybe you yourself have thought this. I once did. But where does the Spirit dwell today? No longer in one temple. Certainly not in multiple buildings. But in believers.

He dwells in believers' bodies (1 Cor. 6:19); our bodies are God's temple. Holy—set apart. And together we make up the stones that comprise the structure built on the foundation of Christ, the apostles, and prophets. We need each other. We are part of the temple not made with hands that exists for the praise of His glory. How can you help build up this "building"?

SATURDAY: CHRIST OUR PEACE

Scripture: "Through Him we both have access in the Spirit to the Father" (Eph. 2:19).

I had never considered myself a racist. When I was kid, my parents helped me send the coins in my piggy bank to Dr. Martin Luther King, Jr.'s work. And I have family members who are African-Americans and Latinos. So, I thought I was good.

I got a glimpse at my blindness when I took Greek from an African-American professor. He told us that racism was not a black-white problem; it was a sin problem. He gave international examples of darker and lighter groups hating each other. Afterward, I said I wanted to be color-blind, and he stopped me. "You need to see the color," he said. "God made it. It's just that the color does not matter in terms of equality." I realized then that my elevating of "blindness" was itself a form of unintentional racism. The very thing God made—the beautiful differences in human melanin—I was priding myself in ignoring outright.

Another glimpse into my own heart came during a trip to the east coast. I had lived in Virginia for seven years as a teen, and at that time, Monticello, home of Thomas Jefferson, was my favorite of the historical sites within a day's drive of Washington, DC. But returning decades later, I was shocked when I saw through fresh eyes the evidence of Jefferson's past as a slaveholder. What upset me most was that his record had not fazed me on my first visit. But I could no longer downplay Jefferson's evil by rationalizing that he was a product of his times. Jefferson knew well the abolitionists' arguments. How could I have been so blind?

I don't know. But between the two above-mentioned instances, some events happened that probably led to some of the scales falling off.

First, I became a Christian. And Jesus changes lives.

Second, I saw the value in hearing from those I'd never really listened to. That started when I took Russian lessons. Only after six weeks' practice could I correctly pronounce the formal word for "hello." I certainly gained a new respect for people trying to speak to me in their second or third or fourth language! I went to Belarus as a journalist with a medical mission team, and my brilliant companions also struggled to speak a language that's actually much easier than English. And also while there, I—a "word" person—had to operate from a vocabulary smaller than a kindergartner's. Suddenly I reconsidered my assessment of the immigrants I had assumed were uneducated.

When I returned, I asked a Russian friend if she had difficulty operating from a limited number of words. She exclaimed, "Yes! That is the hardest part for me being here! In Russia, I am an engineer with an enormous vocabulary. Here, I can hardly express myself." She was an engineer? I had no idea. After that, I started asking about the backgrounds of immigrants who cleaned my office after hours, and I discovered physicians, engineers, and pastors of enormous churches—all sacrificing the respect they received back home in order to have access to Christian education.

When I learned that a theology student was attending a church full of undocumented immigrants, I asked how he could worship with people who were clearly breaking the law just by being here—and he balked. I respected this man, so I wondered aloud how he could view their actions so differently from how I saw them. And He pointed me to Paul's approach with Onesimus, a slave who had fled to Rome illegally. First, Paul shared the gospel, led him to Christ, and helped this runaway law-breaker grow in his faith. And then once Onesimus was mature enough, Paul sent his fellow worker Tychicus back with Onesimus as he sought to comply with the law—even though it meant Onesimus could face death. Paul even used his credentials as an apostle to lean on the master to forgive. (The Book of Philemon in the New Testament is the letter Paul wrote.) I realized my own loyalties were more nationalistic than gospel-focused. That is not to say we encourage law-breaking. Governments must protect their people. But for a Christian interacting with others, first things first. The gospel is the greatest law; even the apostles disobeyed the law if officials enforced it to keep them from preaching the gospel (Acts 5:29).

God loves racial diversity. The music of the ideal day will include every tongue, nation, and tribe worshiping him (Rev. 7:9). That gathering will look like the opposite of Babel, as the nations converge to offer their maker praise. And celebrating racial diversity in our worship foreshadows the coming day. In the words of African Christian Tokunboh Adeyemo, the church is "'the tribe of Jesus'—called out of all tribes and nations but without renouncing those groups." Yet our greater loyalty to Jesus, he says, may at times call for practices and beliefs that override those of one's earthly tribe.[18] Our divisions in the church may no longer be Jew and Gentile. In the west they may be more like Democrat vs. Republican or black, brown, and white. We have different divisions, but we are still divided. And our divisions keep believers from living to the praise of His glory. So we must acknowledge our wrongly ordered priorities; we must share the gospel to bring reconciliation to changed hearts; we must disciple those who have wronged us; we must love our enemies; we must seek to have diverse committees and worship teams and staffs and to attend conferences with a diverse array of speakers, recognizing we don't even know where we are blind. And we must pray that the Lord will grant us sight.

---

18. Tokunboh Adeyemo, *Africa Bible Commentary* (Nairobi, Kenya; Grand Rapids, MI: WordAlive Publishers; Zondervan, 2006), 1456–57.

Ask God to help you to become a beautiful stone that is part of His glorious temple in this hostile and broken world, a temple filled with miracles of Christ-bought unity and shining forth with miracle-working love.

For Memorization: "But God, being rich in mercy, because of his great love with which he loved us, even though we were dead in transgressions, made us alive together with Christ—by grace you are saved—and he raised us up with him and seated us with him in the heavenly realms in Christ Jesus. . . " (Eph. 2:4–6)

Prayer: *Father God, thank you for doing the impossible—taking people who were your enemies and drawing us near; taking people enslaved to sin and setting us free; taking people at war with each other—with legitimate agony from evils done to them—and uniting them in love through Christ. Only your Spirit can work miracles like that. Change my heart, Lord. Help me to see my blindness. Help us to live as one. Help me to glorify you in how I treat my neighbor. In the name of our great peacemaker, Christ the Lord, Amen.*

WEEK 3 OF 6

Belonging: Ephesians 3

Have you ever been in a Christian gathering where week after week members request prayer only for things like their mom's bridge-club friend's son's diabetes? Or their neighbor's dog's wheat allergy? Paul's prayers in the Book of Ephesians and other epistles model a different approach than what we may have heard. He focuses his petitions on heart change: Paul implores God to increase his readers' faith, fill them with hope, grant them wisdom, show them his power, and develop spiritual fruit in their lives. It's not that Paul devalues physical concerns—these are important, too. But Paul's prayers helped his readers fix their eyes on eternal, kingdom values.

Likewise, when Paul asks for prayer for himself, he focuses on using his circumstances to God's glory instead of changing the circumstances themselves (Eph. 6:19–20). Remember that Paul wrote the book of Ephesians from prison. If you were in jail, how would you want people to intercede? Imagine the conditions of a first-century jail: dank, dirty, critter-infested, maybe slithering with snakes, and no flush toilets. Ew-w. I know what I'd ask for! Yet instead of praying for release from jail or health concerns, Paul wanted people to pray he would preach the gospel boldly.

We can model such prayer priorities with our fellow believers too. But (ahem) not so we can act like we're more "spiritual" than they are. As we pray for Aunt Sue's toe surgery, we can also ask that she and those around her might know God's love more deeply and to discern His truths through this trial. As we do so, our own thinking will mature. This kind of intercession invests in God's enduring kingdom. We can still pray for the neighbor's dog—and maybe bring some gluten-free dog treats. But we must bear in mind that we are talking to a great king. How can we most honor him with our requests?

Below you can see a sampling of Paul's prayers for the recipients of his letters. Notice his priorities:

Romans 15:13: Now may the God of hope fill you with all joy and peace as you believe in him, so that you may abound in hope by the power of the Holy Spirit.

Ephesians 1:17–19: I pray that the God of our Lord Jesus Christ, the Father of glory, may give you spiritual wisdom and revelation in your growing knowledge of him,—since the eyes of your heart have been enlightened—so that you may know what is the hope of his calling, what is the wealth of his glorious inheritance in the saints, and what is the incomparable greatness of his power toward us who believe, as displayed in the exercise of his immense strength.

Ephesians 3:16–21: I pray that according to the wealth of his glory he may grant you to be strengthened with power through his Spirit in the inner person, that Christ may dwell in your hearts through faith, so that, because you have been rooted and grounded in love, you may be able to comprehend with all the saints what is the breadth and length and height and depth, and thus to know the love of Christ that surpasses knowledge, so that you may be filled up to all the fullness of God. Now to him who by the power that is working within us is able to do far beyond all that we ask or think, to him be the glory in the church and in Christ Jesus to all generations, forever and ever. Amen.

Philippians 1:9–11: And I pray this, that your love may abound even more and more in knowledge and every kind of insight so that you can decide what is best, and thus be sincere and blameless for the day of Christ, filled with the fruit of righteousness that comes through Jesus Christ to the glory and praise of God.

Colossians 1:9–14: For this reason we also, from the day we heard about you, have not ceased praying for you and asking God to fill you with the knowledge of his will in all spiritual wisdom and understanding, so that you may live worthily of the Lord and please him in all respects—bearing fruit in every good deed, growing in the knowledge of God, being strengthened with all power according to his glorious might for the display of all patience and steadfastness, joyfully giving thanks to the Father who has qualified you to share in the saints' inheritance in the light. He delivered us from the power of darkness and transferred us to the kingdom of the Son he loves, in whom we have redemption, the forgiveness of sins.

1 Thessalonians 5:23–24: Now may the God of peace himself make you completely holy and may your spirit and soul and body be kept entirely blameless at the coming of our Lord Jesus Christ. He who calls you is trustworthy, and he will in fact do this.

2 Thessalonians 1:11–12: And in this regard we pray for you always, that our God will make you worthy of his calling and fulfill by his power your every desire for goodness and every work of faith, that the name of our Lord Jesus may be glorified in you, and you in him, according to the grace of our God and the Lord Jesus Christ.

Philemon 1:6: I pray that the faith you share with us may deepen your understanding of every blessing that belongs to you in Christ.

Do you see Paul's emphasis? Determine to make "not my will but thine be done" the focus of your own prayers and desires, as well.

MONDAY: THE SECRET

1. Pray for wisdom and insight. Then read Ephesians 3. Circle the word "secret" wherever you find it. And remember that back in the previous chapter, Paul had been talking about the uniting of Jew and Gentile into one new man:

Ephesians 3:1 For this reason I, Paul, the prisoner of Christ Jesus for the sake of you Gentiles—**3:2** if indeed you have heard of the stewardship of God's grace that was given to me for you, **3:3** that by revelation the divine secret was made known to me, as I wrote before briefly. **3:4** When reading this, you will be able to understand my insight into this secret of Christ. **3:5** Now this secret was not disclosed to people in former generations as it has now been revealed to his holy apostles and prophets by the Spirit, **3:6** namely, that through the gospel the Gentiles are fellow heirs, fellow members of the body, and fellow partakers of the promise in Christ Jesus. **3:7** I became a servant of this gospel according to the gift of God's grace that was given to me by the exercise of his power. **3:8** To me—less than the least of all the saints—this grace was given, to proclaim to the Gentiles the unfathomable riches of Christ **3:9** and to enlighten everyone about God's secret plan—a secret that has been hidden for ages in God who has created all things. **3:10** The purpose of this enlightenment is that through the church the multifaceted wisdom of God should now be disclosed to the rulers and the authorities in the heavenly realms. **3:11** This was according to the eternal purpose that he accomplished in Christ Jesus our Lord, **3:12** in whom we have boldness and confident access to God because of Christ's faithfulness. **3:13** For this reason I ask you not to lose heart because of what I am suffering for you, which is your glory.

3:14 For this reason I kneel before the Father, **3:15** from whom every family in heaven and on the earth is named. **3:16** I pray that according to the wealth of his glory he may grant you to be strengthened with power through his Spirit in the inner person, **3:17** that Christ may dwell in your hearts through faith, so that, because you have been rooted and grounded in love, **3:18** you may be able to comprehend with all the saints what is the breadth and length and height and depth, **3:19** and thus to know the love of Christ that surpasses knowledge, so that you may be filled up to all the fullness of God.

3:20 Now to him who by the power that is working within us is able to do far beyond all that we ask or think, **3:21** to him be the glory in the church and in Christ Jesus to all generations, forever and ever. Amen.

2. Notice something. See the dash at the end of Ephesians 3:1, and how Paul repeats in verse 14 what he said in vs. 1? Circle both uses of "For this reason I...."

Apparently, Paul, having established the church as comprised of living stones (Eph. 2), begins to pray for his readers (3:1). But he interrupts himself to talk about the secret (vv. 2–13). Once he has done that, he returns to his prayer for them (vv. 14–21).

3. What does Paul have to say about that secret? Underline words in the passage that suggest the secret has been revealed—no longer veiled in mystery.

"**Secret**" (vv. 2, 4, 5, 8)—We usually think of a secret as something unrevealed or undisclosed. But when Paul talks of God's secret here, he is showing how God had plans that in the past He kept to himself, but now He has made His purposes known.

4. What is the actual three-fold content of the mystery (v. 6)?

fellow heirs, fellow members of body, fellow partakers of the promise

> "The mystery mentioned in Ephesians was hidden in God in ages past (3:9). It was something that could not be understood by human ingenuity or study. God revealed it to the apostles and prophets by the Spirit (3:4). Now that it is revealed, it is open to everyone and it is simple to understand and thus not relegated to an intellectual minority. Ephesians views God's sacred secret as believing Jews and Gentiles united into one body. In the OT Gentiles could be a part of the company of God, but they had to become Jews in order to belong to it. In the NT Gentiles do not become Jews nor do Jews become Gentiles. Rather, both believing Jews and Gentiles become one new entity, Christians (Eph. 2:15–16). That is the mystery."
>
> –Harold Hoehner, *Ephesians: An Exegetical Commentary*

TUESDAY: FOCUS ON THE GENTILES

1. Ask the Spirit for insight and read the text for today, Ephesians 3:7–13:

> **Ephesians 3:2** if indeed you have heard of the stewardship of God's grace that was given to me for you, **3:3** that by revelation the divine secret was made known to me, as I wrote before briefly. **3:4** When reading this, you will be able to understand my insight into this secret of Christ. **3:5** Now this secret was not disclosed to people in former generations as it has now been revealed to his holy apostles and prophets by the Spirit, **3:6** namely, that through the gospel the Gentiles are fellow heirs, fellow members of the body,

and fellow partakers of the promise in Christ Jesus. **3:7** I became a servant of this gospel according to the gift of God's grace that was given to me by the exercise of his power. **3:8** To me—less than the least of all the saints—this grace was given, to proclaim to the Gentiles the unfathomable riches of Christ **3:9** and to enlighten everyone about God's secret plan—a secret that has been hidden for ages in God who has created all things. **3:10** The purpose of this enlightenment is that through the church the multifaceted wisdom of God should now be disclosed to the rulers and the authorities in the heavenly realms. **3:11** This was according to the eternal purpose that he accomplished in Christ Jesus our Lord, **3:12** in whom we have boldness and confident access to God because of Christ's faithfulness. **3:13** For this reason I ask you not to lose heart because of what I am suffering for you, which is your glory.

2. How does Paul describe his responsibility to explain the mystery to the Gentiles (v. 2)?

_____

_____

3. Notice the passive "was made known" (v. 3). Who gave the responsibility to Paul?

_____

4. When and to whom was the secret revealed (v. 5)?

_____

_____

We don't know exactly how God revealed Paul's mission to him. Even in A.D. 49, sixteen years after the crucifixion, the Jerusalem church was debating what it meant for Gentiles to be included (Acts 15).

5. Describe Paul's ministry to make known the mystery (vv. 7–13). In today's text, circle Paul's choice of words that emphasize humility (such as "servant") as he describes himself and his awesome stewardship or calling.

_____

6. How does Paul describe what he's preaching, and how does he describe himself (v. 8)?

_____

"The least of all the saints" (v. 8)—This description Paul gives of himself is not some lame effort at false humility. Before Paul became a believer, he was Saul, who blasphemed Christ, persecuted Christ-followers, and tried to utterly destroy the church (see Acts 7:58, 8:1–3, 9:1–8; 26:9–15; 1 Cor. 15:9 Gal 1:13, Phil. 3:6). But God showed grace to him both in opening his heart to the gospel and in calling him as an apostle.

7. Consider the wisdom of God—why do you think God would take a Jewish man with the best of possible Jewish credentials and pedigree, and make him the apostle to the Gentiles?

_____

_____

WEDNESDAY: MANY-COLORED WISDOM

1. Pray for wisdom and insight. Then read Ephesians 3:10–13.

> **3:10** The purpose of this enlightenment is that through the church the multifaceted wisdom of God should now be disclosed to the rulers and the authorities in the heavenly realms. **3:11** This was according to the eternal purpose that he accomplished in Christ Jesus our Lord, **3:12** in whom we have boldness and confident

access to God because of Christ's faithfulness. **3:13** For this reason I ask you not to lose heart because of what I am suffering for you, which is your glory.

2. What does Paul say the church is being used to reveal (v. 10)?

Wisdom of God disclosed to rulers

Do you like to do embroidery? Color in adult coloring books? Flip through a book of art. What activity can you do that involves using many colors? Find such an activity, and as you use your variety of colors, think about the many-colored wisdom of God, especially as it relates to how He has dealt with humans throughout history in so many gracious ways.

"Multifaceted" (v. 10)—The word Paul chooses to describe God's wisdom means "variegated," and it commonly appears throughout classical literature in connection with rich colors alongside each other, as in a field of flowers or a cloth covered with embroidery. Think of Joseph's coat of many colors (see Gen. 37). Or of weavings or your favorite painting. God's wisdom has so many shades and hues and complements and opposites—and so much beauty.

3. To whom and how is God's "variegated" witness revealed (vv. 10–11)?

"Rulers and the authorities in the heavenly realms" (v. 10)— Does Paul mean God's wisdom is being revealed to good angels or evil ones (remember, demons are fallen angels)? Probably both. In Ephesians 1:3, Paul writes of believers' spiritual blessings in the heavenly realms—a good thing. Peter mentions good angels longing but unable to decipher God's plan (1 Pet 1:12). But doubtless, evil angels have been behind much of the animosity between Jew and Gentile.

Yet never would either kind of angel have dreamed that the tension between the two groups would be reconciled in Christ. That God the Son would enrobe himself in human flesh and unite the two groups through violence done to His body? And further, that Gentiles could then inherit the promises given to Abraham's descendants? Who would have thought that would be the plan of God? What a marvel! The church made up of disparate groups loving one another—that is an amazing example of God's many-colored wisdom!

4. What has Christ's faithfulness made possible for those who believe (v. 12)?

_____

5. Paul makes a request. What does he ask from his readers (v. 13)?

_____

6. Paul refers to his sufferings for Gentiles. Based on earlier readings, what sufferings of Paul might have been of concern to his Gentile readers?

_____

7. What is Paul's own view of his suffering (v. 13)?

_____

8. What suffering are you experiencing?

_____

9. Write a prayer asking God to use your suffering for ultimate good. Pray with boldness and confidence in the access you have to God through Christ (v. 12).

_____

1. Pray for wisdom and read Ephesians 3:14-15:

> **Eph. 3:14-15** For this reason I kneel before the Father, from whom every family in heaven and on the earth is named.

"I kneel before the Father" (v. 14)—The apostle has just said believers have access to come before God with boldness (v. 12). And then he proceeds to do so. He describes his physical stance using the verb "kneel" or "bow the knee," which appears only four times in the New Testament: In Romans 11:4, Paul quotes an incident found in the OT in which God tells Elijah that 7,000 men have not bowed the knee to Baal (1 Kings 19:18); in both Romans 14 and Philippians 2, Paul quotes the prophet Isaiah, who recorded that God said every knee will bow and every tongue confess praise to Him (Isa. 45:23); and in our passage here, Paul describes himself as taking a similarly submissive position.

2. Bowing was actually not the typical Jewish way of praying. Circle the bodily stance of people praying in each of these instances:

> Jesus: "Whenever you pray, do not be like the hypocrites, because they love to pray while standing in synagogues and on street corners so that people can see them. Truly I say to you, they have their reward." (Matt. 6:5)

> "The Pharisee stood and prayed about himself like this: 'God, I thank you that I am not like other people . . . ' The tax collector, however, stood far off and would not even look up to heaven, but beat his breast and said, 'God, be merciful to me, sinner that I am!'" (Lk. 18:11-13)

3. Some scholars suggest that when Jewish people knelt, they were doing so out of an expression of deep emotion. Circle the bodily stance of people in the following Bible stories.

Solomon at the dedication of the temple (1 Kgs. 8:54)

> "When Solomon finished presenting all these prayers and requests to the LORD, he got up from before the altar of the LORD where he had knelt and spread out his hands toward the sky"

Stephen at the time of his martyrdom (Acts 7:60)

"Then he fell to his knees and cried out with a loud voice, "Lord, do not hold this sin against them!" When he had said this, he died." (It's possible Stephen falling to his knees was because he was physically unable to stand after being assaulted with stones.)

Peter at the death-bed of Dorcas (Acts 9:40)

"But Peter sent them all outside, knelt down, and prayed. Turning to the body, he said, 'Tabitha, get up.' Then she opened her eyes, and when she saw Peter, she sat up.

Paul at the time of his tear-filled farewells on his last journey to Jerusalem (Acts 20:36; 21:5)

"When he had said these things, he knelt down with them all and prayed."

"When our time was over, we left and went on our way. All of them, with their wives and children, accompanied us outside of the city. After kneeling down on the beach and praying . . ."

Our Lord Himself in Gethsemane in His agony (Luke 22:41)

"He went away from them about a stone's throw, knelt down, and prayed . . ."

We know from art that in the early years of Christianity, believers often prayed with hands raised, elbows bent, palms out.

Iconography from St. Priscilla's catacombs, Rome

Today it is rare for people to pray this way.

Christian denominations have varying practices about one's bodily stance during prayer. But whatever the practice, standing and kneeling are intended as signs of deep respect. If you don't usually lie face-down in prayer, drop to your knees, stand and/or raise your hands, consider doing so in private. Many churches stopped such practices because some began to view them as meaningless ritual. But such does not have to be the case. We can practice prayer in such fashion intentionally, and doing so can provide physical reminders expressed by our bodies that we live in submission to and dependence on God our heavenly Father.

"The Father, from whom every family . . . is named" (vv. 14–15)—It's difficult to see Paul's play on words in English in this phrase, but he prays to the *patera* from whom every *patria* is named. Whether Jew or Gentile, every human has our origin in God our Creator. That means, in one sense, every creature on earth and in heaven has the same Father, whether or not we acknowledge Him. (Yet interestingly, the NT writers limit familial phrases such as "child of God" or "children of God" to those who actually know their Father; we don't see them making statements like "every human is a child of God.")

4. Spend some time praying in adoration. Thank God, the Father of all for His holiness, His sovereignty of all, for creating you, for redeeming you. . . . Consider kneeling, standing, raising hands, or lying face-down as you worship.

FRIDAY: THE SECOND PRAYER IN EPHESIANS

1. Pray for the Spirit's help, and read Ephesians 3:14–21.

Ephesians 3:14 For this reason I kneel before the Father, **3:15** from whom every family in heaven and on the earth is named. **3:16** I pray that according to the wealth of his glory he may grant you to be strengthened with power through his Spirit in the inner person, **3:17** that Christ may dwell in your hearts through faith, so that, because you have been rooted and grounded in love, **3:18** you may be able to comprehend with all the saints what is the breadth and length and height and depth, **3:19** and thus to know the love of Christ that surpasses knowledge, so that you may be filled up to all the fullness of God.

3:20 Now to him who by the power that is working within us is able to do far beyond all that we ask or think, **3:21** to him be the glory in the church and in Christ Jesus to all generations, forever and ever. Amen.

2. Paul writes "for this reason..." (v. 14) a second time. Look back at the previous day's study and try to determine which reason you think he means by "this" when he says "this reason":

---

3. The Trinity is involved in all our spiritual blessings in Christ. God is one in three persons. Circle the differing persons of the Godhead found in vv. 14–17.

4. Paul writes the second prayer we find in the Book of Ephesians. Compare the two prayers below, and contrast the two:

1:17 I pray that the God of our Lord Jesus Christ, the Father of glory, may give you spiritual wisdom and revelation in your growing knowledge of him, **1:18**—since the eyes of your heart have been enlightened—so that you may know what is the hope of his calling, what is the wealth of his glorious inheritance in the saints, **1:19** and what is the incomparable greatness of his power toward us who believe, as displayed in the exercise of his immense strength. **1:20** This power he exercised in Christ when he raised him from the dead and seated him at his right hand in the heavenly realms **1:21** far above every rule and authority and power and dominion and every name that is named, not only in this age but also in the one to come.

3:16 I pray that according to the wealth of his glory he may grant you to be strengthened with power through his Spirit in the inner person, **3:17** that Christ may dwell in your hearts through faith, so that, because you have been rooted and grounded in love, **3:18** you may be able to comprehend with all the saints what is the breadth and length and height and depth, **3:19** and thus to know the love of Christ that surpasses knowledge, so that you may be filled up to all the fullness of God.

3:20 Now to him who by the power that is working within us is able to do far beyond all that we ask or think, **3:21** to him be the glory in the church and in Christ Jesus to all generations, forever and ever. Amen.

What similarities and differences do you find?

_____

_____

5. Circle key words in Paul's two prayers: Christ (4x); glory (3x); know/knowledge (4x); love (2x); power (5x); Spirit/spiritual (2x); strength/strengthened (2x) and wealth (2x). Feel free to use different colored pens or pencils for the different words.

6. Which words appear in both prayers? What might that suggest about Paul's focus on the concepts?

_____

"**Width, length, height and depth**" (v. 18)—When we do a search, we find that biblical authors used the first three of these dimensions (width, length, and height) to describe the ark of the covenant, the Temple, the wisdom of God, and the New Jerusalem—all awesome things. As we come to this passage in Ephesians, Paul has been talking about unity among Jewish and Gentile believers (2:11—3:10). As both groups believed in Jesus as Lord, the first-century church faced a dilemma. Jews despised Gentiles and avoided them at all costs. Yet God planned all along to include the Gentiles in his kingdom (Gen. 12:3; Eph. 1:4, 3:6). Jews and Gentiles co-existing as siblings—that was far beyond all that anyone asked or thought. Their unity shocked those who saw it, and it displayed God's glory through this new church.

> "Thou art coming to a King, large petitions with thee bring, for His grace and power are such none can ever ask too much."
>
> —John Newton

7. Pray through the second prayer for yourself and again for those in your family and church.

SATURDAY: THE FRIEND, THE SPOUSE, THE NEW JOB?

Scripture: "Now to him who by the power that is working within us is able to do far beyond all that we ask or think . . ." (Eph. 3:20).

There's this verse people like to quote a lot. Maybe you've heard it? "Now to him . . . [who] is able to do far beyond all that we ask or think . . ." (Eph. 3:20). The King James wording is "exceedingly, abundantly above. . . ."

Ever asked God to blow your mind with the new job, the spouse He has waiting, or the friendship that needs mending—and tacked on "you can do exceedingly abundantly above all I ask or think"? I have. Yet when I read Ephesians 3:20 more carefully and in context, I realize Paul might mean something different from how we've understood it.

A few verses earlier in the text, Paul prayed for his readers in Asia "that you may be able to comprehend with all the saints what is the breadth and length and height and depth. . . " (v. 18). But breadth, length, height, and depth of what? He does not say specifically.

Many scholars believe "breadth, length, height, and depth" (v. 18) refer to the love of Christ. After all, the verse is sandwiched between two references to love. Verse 17 before it ends with "grounded in love," and verse 19 after it picks up with "and thus to know the love of Christ." The New International Version (NIV) even translates the verse "how wide and long and high and deep is the love of Christ," adding the object of comprehension (the love of Christ) for us. But that isn't in the original Greek. (Still, it does not hurt to pray that we would comprehend the width, length, height, and depth of Christ's love!)

If so, in saying God can do "far beyond," Paul was not talking in general about God blowing our minds with cool events. In fact, Paul said the amazing things will happen "by the power that is working within us." So rather than looking externally, Paul wants readers to see what God does inside believers. The same power that raised Christ from the dead (Eph. 1:19–20) changes our hearts, even when we don't know to ask or think about it. The worst prejudices melt into love. Indeed, the real miracle is that through Christ, God gives us the ability to forgive those who trespass against us and love others who differ from us—even those with whom we've experienced shared animosity. Through the church, God displays his transforming work. He changes lives. Radically. To him be the glory!

P.S. He is able to exceedingly, abundantly work beyond all we ask or think in any area. So, keep asking, seeking, knocking. And keep expecting Him to do miracles with jobs and spouses and friends. Just know that the verse was talking about God's ability to bring love where hatred existed. We need to make sure that's our prayer priority, too!

For Memorization: "I pray that according to the wealth of his glory he may grant you to be strengthened with power through his Spirit in the inner person, that Christ may dwell in your hearts through faith, so that, because you have been rooted and grounded in love, you may be able to comprehend with all the saints what is the breadth and length and height and depth, and thus to know the love of Christ that surpasses knowledge, so that you may be filled up to all the fullness of God" (Eph. 3:16–19).

Prayer: *Gracious heavenly Father, I pray that according to the wealth of your glory that you might grant me to be strengthened with power through your Spirit in the inner person, that Christ may dwell in my heart through faith, so that, because I have been rooted and grounded in love, I may be able to comprehend with all the saints what is the breadth and length and height and depth, and thus to know the love of Christ that surpasses knowledge, so that I may be filled up to all your fullness. I ask this for members of my church and for my family as well. In the name of Christ, Amen.*

Week 4 of 6

New and Diverse: Ephesians 4

In his letter to the Ephesians, Paul mentions a purpose for Christ's descending to earth and ascending to heaven: "that he might fill all things" (4:10). And in this age, how does the Lord fill all things? Through us—the body of Christ, that is, "the fulness of him who fills all in all" (1:23). God does so by equipping believers to do such "filling": "And he gave some, apostles; and some, prophets; and some, evangelists; and some, pastors and teachers; to equip the saints for the work of the ministry, that is, to build up the body of Christ" (4:10–12).

When we believe, the Spirit gives each of us at least one gift to use for equipping other believers to minister, to build up Christ's body. Note what Paul said is the gifts' purpose: not personal glory or even the sole benefit of one's biological family, but for the building up of the body of Christ. Do you notice it's not the paid vocational minister's job to build up the body and do ministry, but every Christian's?

As he loves to do, Paul uses a metaphor of a physical body. In Christ's body, each person is a "member" in the same way fingers, eyes, and ears belong to a physical body. The whole is the church; and individuals are members. Every member needs every part to make up a healthy, mature body. Consequently, we need others who have what we lack; but others need us too, so they won't lack.

Both Paul and Peter list spiritual gifts in their writings besides those mentioned in Ephesians 4, including prophecy, serving, teaching, exhortation, giving, leadership, mercy (Rom. 12:6–8), words of wisdom, words of knowledge, faith, gifts of healings, miracles, prophecy, discerning spirits, tongues, and interpretation of tongues (1 Cor. 12:8–10); and speaking and helps (1 Pet. 4:11).

Back in Paul's list in Ephesians (4:10–12), did you notice the plural of "pastors and teachers" (4:11)? "Pastor" means "shepherd," and it's a spiritual gift, not an office. (Paul certainly does not have in mind anything like a CEO or an organization chart when he speaks of "pastor.")

We must distinguish a spiritual gift from an office. We sometimes get the idea that each congregation has only one person with the office of pastor. But pastor is not an office (elder, widow, deacon, female deacon—these are the words that appear in contexts that speak of offices–e.g., 1 Tim. 1:1; 3:8, 11; 5:9–10). Each local gathering of believers has multiple people, men and women, with a variety of gifts, including those who shepherd others.

What do you think your gift is (or gifts are)? What are ways in which others say you bless them? Ask God to help you use your gifts, even if you're not sure what they are, to build up the body of Christ, helping it come to maturity.

MONDAY: SO WHAT?

We can divide Paul's letter of the Ephesians pretty evenly into two halves. The first half, which we just finished studying, lays out who we are and what God has done for us. The second half begins with "I, therefore . . ." And an old principle of studying literature is that when we see the word "therefore," we should find out what it's there for. And, in the case of Paul's letters, that usually means reminding ourselves of what has just been argued. In this case, Paul is taking all that great information about the lordship of Christ and our spiritual blessings and identity as God's children with access to Him and our oneness with one another—and now Paul's delivering the "so what." What difference does it make? What should we do about it? How should we therefore live? In light of who God is, all He has done for us, the Jew/Gentile union in Christ, our purpose to be "to the praise of His glory," and so much more, we now consider what difference it should make.

1. Pray for the Holy Spirit's insight. Then read Ephesians 4:

> **Ephesians 4:1** I, therefore, the prisoner for the Lord, urge you to live worthily of the calling with which you have been called, **4:2** with all humility and gentleness, with patience, bearing with one another in love, **4:3** making every effort to keep the unity of the Spirit in the bond of peace. **4:4** There is one body and one Spirit, just as you too were called to the one hope of your calling, **4:5** one Lord, one faith, one baptism, **4:6** one God and Father of all, who is over all and through all and in all.
>
> **4:7** But to each one of us grace was given according to the measure of the gift of Christ. **4:8** Therefore it says, "When he ascended on high he captured captives; he gave gifts to men." **4:9** Now what is the meaning of "he ascended," except that he also descended to the lower regions, namely, the earth? **4:10** He, the very one who descended, is also the one who ascended above all the heavens, in order to fill all things. **4:11** It was he who gave some as apostles, some as prophets, some as evangelists, and some as pastors and teachers, **4:12** to equip the saints for the work of ministry, that is, to build up the body of Christ, **4:13** until we all attain to the unity of the faith and of the knowledge of the Son of God—a mature person, attaining to the measure of Christ's full stature. **4:14** So we are no longer to be children, tossed back and forth by waves and carried about by every wind of teaching by the trickery of people who craftily carry out their deceitful schemes. **4:15** But practicing the truth in love, we will in all things grow up into Christ, who is the head. **4:16** From him the whole body grows, fitted and held together through every supporting ligament. As each one does its part, the body grows in love.
>
> **4:17** So I say this, and insist in the Lord, that you no longer live as the Gentiles do, in the futility of their thinking. **4:18** They are darkened in their understanding, being alienated from the life of God because of the ignorance that is in them due to the hardness of their hearts. **4:19** Because they are callous, they have given themselves over to indecency for the practice of every kind of impurity with greediness. **4:20** But you did not learn about Christ like this, **4:21** if indeed you heard about him and were taught in him, just as the truth is in Jesus. **4:22** You were taught with reference to your

former way of life to lay aside the old man who is being corrupted in accordance with deceitful desires, **4:23** to be renewed in the spirit of your mind, **4:24** and to put on the new man who has been created in God's image—in righteousness and holiness that comes from truth.

4:25 Therefore, having laid aside falsehood, each one of you speak the truth with his neighbor, for we are members of one another. **4:26** Be angry and do not sin; do not let the sun go down on the cause of your anger. **4:27** Do not give the devil an opportunity. **4:28** The one who steals must steal no longer; rather he must labor, doing good with his own hands, so that he may have something to share with the one who has need. **4:29** You must let no unwholesome word come out of your mouth, but only what is beneficial for the building up of the one in need, that it may give grace to those who hear. **4:30** And do not grieve the Holy Spirit of God, by whom you were sealed for the day of redemption. **4:31** You must put away all bitterness, anger, wrath, quarreling, and slanderous talk—indeed all malice. **4:32** Instead, be kind to one another, compassionate, forgiving one another, just as God in Christ also forgave you.

2. What recurring ideas do you notice? What does he stress?

_____

_____

_____

TUESDAY: ONE. ONE. ONE.

1. Pray for wisdom and read Ephesians 4:1–6

Ephesians 4:1: I, therefore, the prisoner for the Lord, urge you to live worthily of the calling with which you have been called, **4:2** with all humility and gentleness, with patience, bearing with one another in love, **4:3** making every effort to keep the unity of the Spirit in the bond of peace. **4:4** There is one body and one Spirit, just as you too were called to the one hope of your calling, **4:5** one

Lord, one faith, one baptism, **4:6** one God and Father of all, who is over all and through all and in all.

2. Circle the four forms of the word "call" in this passage.

3. Underline the word "one." In the first occurrence it is used as part of a term "one another." But in every other use, the emphasis is on the numeral one.

4. How many times does Paul use the word "one" in vv. 4–6?

_____

5. Circle references to members of the Trinity. The three persons of the Godhead work together as one in our lives and relationships. (Often when a biblical author talks about "the Lord," he has Christ in mind.)

"The prisoner for the Lord" (4:1)—Paul is a prisoner because he was arrested due to his gospel ministry among the Gentiles—a great example of putting others' needs before his own. (Eventually he will die for his choice to do so.) His willingness to sit in prison for his faith gives him credibility to call other believers to live in a worthy way.

"Live worthily" (v. 1)—Paul urges readers to "walk worthy." The word translated here as "worthily" literally means to "bring up under the beam of a scale." So picture a scale with a balance beam in which both sides would equal each other. There should be no imbalance between our calling in Christ and the way we live our lives.

"The calling with which you have been called" (v. 1)—Paul had mentioned God's "calling" back in 1:18, where he prayed his readers would know "what is the hope of his calling . . ." Although our first thought when we hear the word "calling" is usually one's vocation, that is not what Paul is talking about. Instead of asking, "What job does God want me to do?" we should ask "Who should I be?" In this verse and elsewhere in the New Testament, "calling" is connected with the believer's election (see Eph. 1:18, 4:1, 4, and also Rom. 11:29; 2 Thess. 1:11; and Heb. 3:1). In Ephesians, calling is also connected with the believer's union in Christ's body, the church. So instead of thinking tasks here, think character and interpersonal relationships. Paul goes on to give examples of what that looks like.

6. Look at verses 2 and 3. What hints do you get from the passage that when Paul speaks of our calling he has our conformity to Christ (or our character) in mind in the context of interpersonal relationships?

_____

_____

7. In what five ways does Paul envision his readers walking worthily (vv. 2–3)?

•

•

•

•

•

"Bearing with one another in love" (v. 2)—Or more literally, "forbearing one another in love." Such "bearing" carries the idea of enduring. Jesus used it when He asked how long He should bear with the disciples (Matt. 17:17), and Paul spoke of enduring persecution (1 Cor. 4:12). Love is a marvelous concept, but it's much more difficult to live it than talk about it.

8. Think about who gets on your last nerve. Or what people group you have trouble caring for. Do you ever think, I'm so done being kind to that person? Ask the Spirit to grant you not just tolerance, but forbearance in love.

"Making every effort to keep the unity of the Spirit in the bond of peace" (v. 3)—Notice in verse 3 Paul says to keep or preserve what already exists. Notice, too, that he says, "make every effort to." He does not say to keep the peace. He says to try (Rom. 12:18). Sometimes despite all we've done, we can do no more. But unity is essential and requires every possible effort.

9. Paul goes on to emphasize the work of the Trinity in our oneness. In Jewish thought the number seven was the number of perfection. Notice Paul's seven "ones":

1. One body: He's been discussing the body of Christ, the church, throughout. Believers are members of one universal body.
2. One Spirit: The Holy Spirit. One body, and one Spirit are connected. The Spirit unites us.
3. To one hope of your calling: Paul laid out his readers' future hope in chapter 1—remember? The believer's future reality is the hope of their glorious inheritance in a united earth and heaven.
4. One Lord: a reference to Christ. Through His physical body, the union of Jews and Gentiles into one body is made possible.
5. One faith: In the previous chapter Paul has laid out salvation by grace alone through faith alone in Jesus Christ.
6. One baptism: Some see this as a reference to water baptism; that may be. But because Paul has focused so much in Ephesians on the believer's identity through Christ's death, it seems probable that he means the identification of the believer with Christ's death and burial at the time of salvation.
7. One God and Father of all, who is over all and through all and in all: As Paul had said, God is the father of every family in heaven and earth (3:15). Although God is three persons—Father, Son, and Holy Spirit—He is one.

10. Write a poem, prayer, or rap that incorporates these seven essentials of our oneness in Christ.

WEDNESDAY: GRACE GIFTS

1. Pray for wisdom and read Ephesians 4:7–16.

> **Ephesians 4:7** But to each one of us grace was given according to the measure of the gift of Christ. **4:8** Therefore it says, "When he ascended on high he captured captives; he gave gifts to men."

4:9 Now what is the meaning of "he ascended," except that he also descended to the lower regions, namely, the earth? **4:10** He, the very one who descended, is also the one who ascended above all the heavens, in order to fill all things. **4:11** It was he who gave some as apostles, some as prophets, some as evangelists, and some as pastors and teachers, **4:12** to equip the saints for the work of ministry, that is, to build up the body of Christ, **4:13** until we all attain to the unity of the faith and of the knowledge of the Son of God—a mature person, attaining to the measure of Christ's full stature. **4:14** So we are no longer to be children, tossed back and forth by waves and carried about by every wind of teaching by the trickery of people who craftily carry out their deceitful schemes. **4:15** But practicing the truth in love, we will in all things grow up into Christ, who is the head. **4:16** From him the whole body grows, fitted and held together through every supporting ligament. As each one does its part, the body grows in love.

2. According to v. 7, who receives grace gifts?

_____

"Grace was given" (4:7)—In New Testament contexts where spiritual gifts appear, we usually find the concept of "grace." One of God's graces to the church is His equipping each of us with a gift or gifts of the Spirit for edification of the body. Notice that the work of ministry is not the task of some paid clergy member, but the job of every believer.

3. Complete this sentence: I think my spiritual gift(s) is (are)

_____.

"He ascended . . . and gave gifts" (v. 8)—Here Paul alludes to Psalm 68:18. The psalm celebrates how God has overcome Israel's enemies in battle and pictures Him as a conquering king, ascending Mt. Sinai after a victory:

> You ascend on high,
>
> You have taken many captives.
>
> You receive tribute from men,
>
> Including even sinful rebels (Psa. 68:18)

Paul paints an updated version of this image of God as the conquering hero, this time with Jesus as conqueror. Paul starts this picture by describing the ultimate triumph over one's enemies (Jesus' death and resurrection), transitions to Christ's ultimate ascension on high—the ascension (Acts 1:9–10; Eph. 4:10), and then concludes with an introduction to the spiritual gifts. In Paul's vision, Christ is such an awesome conqueror that instead of receiving tribute, He distributes victory gifts. And these gifts help the body of Christ mature.

4. In the body diagram above, write "Christ" on the head (v. 14).

5. Fill in some details—eyes, ears, mouth, nose, fingers, toes. . . . Then write the names of the spiritual gifts Paul lists (v. 11) on different parts of the body.

6. What does Paul say is the purpose of such gifts (hint: it's not popularity, attention, one-upping, lording over . . .) (v. 12)?

_____

7. In this analogy, when does Christ reach full stature (v. 13)?

_____

_____

_____

8. What behavior is immature (v. 14)?

_____

9. What behavior is growth-producing (v. 15)?

_____

10. What enables the body to grow in love (v. 16)?

_____

11. Share a time when someone told you the truth in love.

_____

_____

_____

_____

12. What is the danger to the church's maturity if we tell the truth without love?

13. What is the danger to the church's maturity if we love without telling the truth?

14. Who needs you to tell them the truth in love?

THURSDAY: PUT OFF, PUT ON

1. Pray for wisdom and read Eph. 4:17–24:

> **Ephesians 4:17** So I say this, and insist in the Lord, that you no longer live as the Gentiles do, in the futility of their thinking. **4:18** They are darkened in their understanding, being alienated from the life of God because of the ignorance that is in them due to the hardness of their hearts. **4:19** Because they are callous, they have given themselves over to indecency for the practice of every kind of impurity with greediness. **4:20** But you did not learn about Christ like this, **4:21** if indeed you heard about him and were taught in him, just as the truth is in Jesus. **4:22** You were taught with reference to your former way of life to lay aside the old man [person] who is being corrupted in accordance with deceitful desires, **4:23** to be renewed in the spirit of your mind, **4:24** and to put on the new man [person] who has been created in God's image—in righteousness and holiness that comes from truth.

That was then, this is now...

2. Previously in his letter, Paul spoke of one new person—comprised of Jew and Gentile (Eph. 2:15). Now he is going to talk about "one new person" again, but this time Paul will contrast two people that are

not united. In fact, they could not be further apart. Circle references above to these two people in vv. 22–24.

3. Notice how much "understanding," "thinking," and "mind" (three words Paul uses to refer to our thoughts) affect behavior. Underline words that relate to how one thinks.

4. Circle references to falsehood and truth.

5. How does Paul say his readers formerly lived? Notice how their thinking led to specific behaviors.

_____

_____

6. What three things have Paul's readers rightly been taught to do with their former way of life (vv. 22–23)?

•

•

•

7. Every human is created in the image of God (Gen. 1:26–27). But this image was corrupted by the Fall. Yet in Christ, believers have been created anew in that image. How does Paul describe that image (v. 24)?

_____

8. What are some ways you can renew your mind with truth? With what are you filling your mind? What lies do you tell yourself and/or believe? In what ways are you already doing well filling your mind with good things? How can you fill your mind with more truth? Podcasts? Messages? Music? Media?

_____

_____

_____

FRIDAY: THE WAY WE TALK

1. Pray for insight and read Ephesians 4:25–32.

> **Ephesians 4:25** Therefore, having laid aside falsehood, each one of you speak the truth with his neighbor, for we are members of one another. **4:26** Be angry and do not sin; do not let the sun go down on the cause of your anger. **4:27** Do not give the devil an opportunity. **4:28** The one who steals must steal no longer; rather he must labor, doing good with his own hands, so that he may have something to share with the one who has need. **4:29** You must let no unwholesome word come out of your mouth, but only what is beneficial for the building up of the one in need, that it may give grace to those who hear. **4:30** And do not grieve the Holy Spirit of God, by whom you were sealed for the day of redemption. **4:31** You must put away all bitterness, anger, wrath, quarreling, and slanderous talk—indeed all malice. **4:32** Instead, be kind to one another, compassionate, forgiving one another, just as God in Christ also forgave you.

2. Righteousness is not the absence of sinful behavior. It is the presence of just and beautiful behavior. Thus, Paul tells his readers what behaviors to get rid of and the beautiful behaviors to replace the old stuff with—and why or in what way. Complete this chart to get a visual picture of Paul's advice.

Verses	Lay aside this	Replace with this	Rationale
v. 25			
vv. 26–27			
v. 28			
v. 29			
vv. 30–32			

3. In what way do you think harboring wrath gives the devil an opportunity (v. 27)?

_____

"He must labor, doing good with his own hands, so that he
. . ." (v. 28)—The male pronouns here give the impression that Paul
had in mind a male thief/laborer. But the Greek has no specific sex in
view. Frankly, it's awkward in English to write that the one who steals
must work at doing good with that person's own hands so that such
a person will have. . . . Yet that is the idea here. One of my favorite
Greek professors and I got into a conversation about this one day, and
he later emailed me to jokingly say that if male-emphasis translations
were correct, "I guess Paul would have been okay with *Oceans 8*, but
not with *Oceans 11, 12,* or *13.*" A woman who pilfers, steals, shoplifts,
and/or embezzles needs to work with the very appendages she has
used to commit the crime—her hands—so she can use those appendages to do the opposite of stealing, which is to give away what she has
worked to obtain.

4. In what way is sharing something we've made with someone in
need a brilliant and beautiful alternative to stealing?

_____

5. What are some contexts in which you're tempted to use words that
tear down instead of giving grace? (Keep in mind that grace is unmerited favor—people may not deserve our kind words.) In a literate
society, the words may come from what we write in addition to what
we say. Ask the Spirit to help you limit your communication to ways
that build up and give grace.

_____

6. Marie Wilkinson's father-in-law escaped slavery. After she was
awarded the prestigious Lumen Christi Award in 2002, she said, "You
can get angry at the things people do, but you can't hate any person."
Grasping the torture whip she inherited from her father-in-law, she

said, "I take this whip, and I teach a lot of people not to hate." Who are you tempted to hate? Ask God to love your enemies through you.

7. Paul speaks of grieving the Holy Spirit of God (v. 30). This detail reveals something important about God. The Father, Son, and Holy Spirit are persons with personalities. God feels joy and pain, love and grief. The Holy Spirit has sealed each believer, indwelling us. Which means when we sin, we take him with us. Ask the Spirit to search your heart for ways you grieve him and repent.

SATURDAY: AS WE FORGIVE THOSE...

Scripture: Be kind to one another, compassionate, forgiving one another, just as God in Christ also forgave you (Eph. 4:32).

Years ago, I wrote the script for an Easter musical in which my husband was cast in the part of Jesus; I myself played the part of an "extra" in the choir/crowd.

We were well into production when the director (my brother in Christ) announced he was adding a scene—one with a demon-possessed man. And then this director dropped a bomb: the new character would enter screaming like a wild man—and dressed as caveman Fred Flintstone.

I thought the decision was in poor taste, so I went to the director privately and appealed to him to reconsider. I felt the scene detracted from the solemnity we were going for in the scene, and because my name was on the program as the writer, I also hated for people to think it was my own creation.

The director's response? He set his jaw and told me to live with it.

Reeling from the shock, I proceeded to dress rehearsal. As I sang and acted out my part, I struggled to know the best way to handle the situation. I was livid with my brother, but I also knew better than to rally everyone against him. Should I quietly go home? Approach his boss? Try again to talk with him? Try to let it go? I didn't know. But what I did know was that I felt angry and bitter.

We were singing about the Via Dolorosa, the Way of Suffering in Old Jerusalem, believed to be the path Jesus took to the crucifixion, when my husband entered. And he was dressed—or in this case, nearly undressed—in character as Jesus, covered with blood and bruises, and his head crowned with three-inch thorns that dripped with more blood running down his cheeks. Carrying a heavy cross, he could barely hold up his head. And the sight of this much-loved-to-me man so violently altered by torture made me catch my breath, blink back tears, and swallow hard.

And then I saw past the face of my husband to the person he was portraying, Jesus Christ.

Who had committed the worse offense—my brother who had wrecked my drama or I, whose sins sent Jesus to the cross to bear them in my stead? These words came to my mind: "Be kind to one another, compassionate, forgiving one another, just as God in Christ also forgave you" (Eph. 4:32). That is the point of Paul's words. If Christ could forgive us for sending him to a violent death for us, what lesser offense shall we not forgive?

Regardless of what else I did about the conflict, I knew the first thing I had to do was forgive.

Now, I am only a mere kindergartner in the school of forgiveness. But my friend Celestín is a graduate. In the early years following the Rwandan genocide, revenge killings continued. One day, uniformed men descended on his village and murdered seventy people, including his stepbrother and his father.

After that, Celestín had to make a choice. He could either, as he described it, "fail to forgive and lead a life without freedom, joy, and peace," or he could forgive his enemy as Christ had done with him.

Celestín chose to forgive—a choice that required not a one-time decision but a daily one. But that was not the end. Sometime later, Celestín was training pastors when he discovered among his students three relatives of the men who murdered his loved ones. The rage was real; how he loathed these people! But again, the Spirit reminded Celestín of his decision to forgive. And that day he repented before them and asked their forgiveness. Their response? They asked Celestín to forgive them on behalf of their family. Much weeping, public confession, and forgiveness followed. Then other leaders who also harbored hatred and bitterness publicly repented.

The words "Forgive as Christ forgave you" often appear inscribed on decorative calendars and cute plaques. But actually living in obedience to this command is quite another story.

Are you holding a grudge? Harboring anger and bitterness? Has someone violated or offended you or someone you love, and you want revenge? Has Christ forgiven you? Will you forgive?

For Memorization: "Be kind to one another, compassionate, forgiving one another, just as God in Christ also forgave you" (Eph. 4:32).

Prayer: *Father, forgive us our trespasses as we forgive those who trespass against us. In Jesus name, Amen.*

Week 5 of 6

Spirit Filled: Ephesians 5

Sunday: Filling Big Shoes

Scripture: "Therefore, be imitators of God as dearly loved children and live in love, just as Christ also loved us and gave himself for us, a sacrificial and fragrant offering to God" (Eph. 5:1-2).

When she was a little girl, my friend Angela loved to wear her mother's shoes. Angela recalls,

> "Mom often found me clomping through the house in whatever pair she had lying around. When her belly grew with my brother, I shoved stuffed animals in my shirt to create a bulge of my own. After he was born, I soothed and fed my doll, just like Mom did with her living, breathing baby. I begged to smear her lipstick on my lips, but with my untrained hand, I looked less like her than like Ronald McDonald.
>
> "My three-year-old self couldn't articulate it, but I imitated Mom because I felt secure in her love. I spent time with her and watched her closely. I never doubted her affection. When I sulked in 'time out' for hitting my brother, I knew Mom's

unwavering love held steady. Her foundation of love gave me courage to make friends, discover my personality, and take the training wheels off my bike."

Do you have similar memories of imitation? Maybe not with a parent, but trying to act like a "big kid" when you were little? That's what Paul tells us to do with our loving Lord: "Therefore, be imitators of God as dearly loved children and live in love, just as Christ also loved us and gave himself for us, a sacrificial and fragrant offering to God" (Eph. 5:1). Paul cites specific actions our new life in Christ should take on, like honesty, sexual purity, and kindness (Eph. 4–5).

What does it mean to live in love (5:1)? The word for "loved" means beloved, esteemed, the favorite. The same word is used when God calls Jesus His "beloved Son" (Matt. 3:17). Nothing can separate us from God's love (Rom. 8:39). Through our faith in Christ, we get to be called God's children (Gal. 3:26). As His kids, then, we live knowing God loves us with the same love He has for Jesus! And each of us is God's beloved child. Sit and meditate on that for a moment.

Only this love that surpasses knowledge (3:19) can change our hearts and behaviors. The foundation God lays with His love makes us secure, and we begin imitating Him. But instead of shoes, baby dolls, and lipstick, our imitation of God shows itself in our love for others. As we spend time with Him, we know Him more intimately. Truth, patience, and generosity pour out of us, not as items on a "To do" list, but because our Father acts this way, and we want to be just like Him.

MONDAY: THE BIG PICTURE

1. Pray for the Holy Spirit's insight. Then read Ephesians 5

> **Ephesians 5:1** Therefore, be imitators of God as dearly loved children **5:2** and live in love, just as Christ also loved us and gave himself for us, a sacrificial and fragrant offering to God. **5:3** But among you there must not be either sexual immorality, impurity of any kind, or greed, as these are not fitting for the saints. **5:4** Neither should there be vulgar speech, foolish talk, or coarse jesting—all of which are out of character—but rather thanksgiving. **5:5** For you can be confident of this one thing: that no person who is immoral, impure, or greedy (such a person is an idolater) has any inheritance in the kingdom of Christ and God.

5:6 Let nobody deceive you with empty words, for because of these things God's wrath comes on the sons of disobedience. **5:7** Therefore do not be partakers with them, **5:8** for you were at one time darkness, but now you are light in the Lord. Walk as children of the light—**5:9** for the fruit of the light consists in all goodness, righteousness, and truth—**5:10** trying to learn what is pleasing to the Lord. **5:11** Do not participate in the unfruitful deeds of darkness, but rather expose them. **5:12** For the things they do in secret are shameful even to mention. **5:13** But all things being exposed by the light are made evident. **5:14** For everything made evident is light, and for this reason it says:

"Awake, O sleeper!
Rise from the dead,
and Christ will shine on you!"

5:15 Therefore be very careful how you live—not as unwise but as wise, **5:16** taking advantage of every opportunity, because the days are evil. **5:17** For this reason do not be foolish, but be wise by understanding what the Lord's will is. **5:18** And do not get drunk with wine, which is debauchery, but be filled by the Spirit, **5:19** speaking to one another in psalms, hymns, and spiritual songs, singing and making music in your hearts to the Lord, **5:20** always giving thanks to God the Father for each other in the name of our Lord Jesus Christ, **5:21** and submitting to one another out of reverence for Christ.

5:22 Wives, submit to your husbands as to the Lord, **5:23** because the husband is the head of the wife as also Christ is the head of the church—he himself being the savior of the body. **5:24** But as the church submits to Christ, so also wives should submit to their husbands in everything. **5:25** Husbands, love your wives just as Christ loved the church and gave himself for her **5:26** to sanctify her by cleansing her with the washing of the water by the word, **5:27** so that he may present the church to himself as glorious—not having a stain or wrinkle, or any such blemish, but holy and blameless. **5:28** In the same way husbands ought to love their wives as their own bodies. He who loves his wife loves himself. **5:29** For no one has ever hated his own body but he feeds it and takes care of it, just as Christ also does the church, **5:30** for we are members of his body. **5:31** For this reason a man will leave his father and mother and will be joined to his wife, and the two will become one flesh. **5:32** This mystery is great—but I am actually speaking with reference to Christ and the church. **5:33** Nevertheless, each one of you must also love his own wife as he loves himself, and the wife must respect her husband.

2. What stands out to you as you read?

_____

_____

_____

_____

3. What questions does this passage raise for you?

_____

_____

_____

TUESDAY: IMITATION OF LIFE

1. Pray for the Spirit's help. Then read Ephesians 5:1–5.

> **Ephesians. 5:1** Therefore, be imitators of God as dearly loved children **5:2** and live in love, just as Christ also loved us and gave himself for us, a sacrificial and fragrant offering to God. **5:3** But among you there must not be either sexual immorality, impurity of any kind, or greed, as these are not fitting for the saints. **5:4** Neither should there be vulgar speech, foolish talk, or coarse jesting—all of which are out of character—but rather thanksgiving. **5:5** For you can be confident of this one thing: that no person who is immoral, impure, or greedy (such a person is an idolater) has any inheritance in the kingdom of Christ and God.

2. What are some of your favorite fragrances—for example, perfumes or colognes, campfires, burgers on the grill?

_____

_____

3. What aroma was pleasing to God (v. 2)?

_____

4. How does the kind of love (*agapē*) seen in Christ differ from that of our natural impulses?

_____

5. Who needs you to show the *agapē* kind of love, and how?

_____

6. Paul describes two ways of living—a negative one full of vices that are inconsistent with our identity, and a positive one full of beautiful virtues that replace the vices. Fill in the columns below with behaviors to put off and the one to put on:

Things not fitting for saints (vv. 3–4)	What is fitting (v. 4)
Sexual immorality	thanksgiving
impurity	
greed	
vulgar speech	

"Vulgar speech, foolish talk, or coarse jesting" (v. 4)—A Christian's talk should sound different from the speech of those who live in darkness. Vulgar speech takes what God made as beautiful—human sexuality, for example—and cheapens it. "Foolish talk," according to Plutarch the first-century Greek biographer, was the type of nonsense that comes from the lips of a drunk person: it neither makes sense nor profits anyone. Also forbidden is coarse jesting. The idea is that whatever is said might be quite funny, but it crosses the line of propriety. Once again, Paul makes a play on words: replace *eutrapelia* by *eucharistia*—or replace the grace of a certain kind of rankness with the grace of thankfulness.

7. In what areas and/or contexts does your speech need to better align with your new identity, as you walk worthy of your calling?

_____

_____

8. A thankful heart is congruent with a Christian's new identity (v. 5). List some things for which you are thankful.

_____

_____

_____

_____

_____

"Inheritance in the kingdom of Christ and God" (v. 5)—Paul has talked a lot about the believer's inheritance, and he has been careful to disconnect it from the works we do. He seems to suggest here that we should not assume the person who lives a life of immorality, greed, idolatry, or impurity is a child of God. This is not to say someone must give up these things to receive eternal life. Rather, the person who truly believes in Christ has a new nature and identity and abhors such things. If we love such things, we should search our hearts to make sure we are in Christ.

Statistics show that women are struggling with porn addiction in our churches. Check out the stats: one out of every three visitors to an adult site is a woman; seventeen percent of women struggle with pornography addiction[1]. Sixty to eighty percent of women struggle at some time in their life with masturbation. And about seventy percent of women keep their sexual addictions secret. If you struggle with such compulsions, find an accountability partner. Studies on addiction affirm our need to live in community. The Holy Spirit empowers, and part of His means of giving us victory is through the support of other believers, fellow members of Christ's body.

19. Joy Pedrow Skarka, "Why the Church Needs to Address Porn Addiction for Women." http://joypedrow.com/2016/06/why-the-church-needs-to-address-porn-addiction-for-women/ accessed July 7, 2018.

9. Ask the Spirit to search your heart for any immorality, impurity and/or greediness. Repent—which means doing a 180-degree turn with the help of the Spirit.

WEDNESDAY: LIVE IN THE LIGHT

1. Pray for the Spirit's help. Then read Ephesians 5:6–14.

Ephesians 5:6 Let nobody deceive you with empty words, for because of these things God's wrath comes on the sons of disobedience. **5:7** Therefore do not be partakers with them, **5:8** for you were at one time darkness, but now you are light in the Lord. Walk as children of the light—**5:9** for the fruit of the light consists in all goodness, righteousness, and truth—**5:10** trying to learn what is pleasing to the Lord. **5:11** Do not participate in the unfruitful deeds of darkness, but rather expose them. **5:12** For the things they do in secret are shameful even to mention. **5:13** But all things being exposed by the light are made evident. **5:14** For everything made evident is light, and for this reason it says:

"Awake, O sleeper!
Rise from the dead,
and Christ will shine on you!"

2. What are the "these things" to which Paul is referring (v. 6)—things which are consistent with being sons of disobedience and that incur God's wrath?

_____

3. What are Paul's imperatives (commands) in the passage that relate to such behavior (vv. 6, 7, 10, 11)?

_____

_____

4. Paul contrasts his readers' old identity and their new identity (v. 8) as the logic behind why they should be different now.

Whom does he say they used to be (v. 8)? _____

Whom does he say they are now (v. 8)? _____

5. What is the evidence (fruit) in the lives of children of light (v. 9)?

_____

6. Instead of participating in works of darkness, we are to do more than avoid them. What is our task (v. 11)?

_____

7. Why (vv. 12, 13)?

_____

8. Are there deeds of darkness you need to expose? And if so, how?

Paul closes this section with what he has probably borrowed from an early Christian hymn. If so, he is doing what he will shortly instruct his readers to do: speak to one another in psalms, hymns, and spiritual songs (5:19):

> "Awake, O sleeper!
> Rise from the dead,
> and Christ will shine on you!"

In this short piece of poetic truth, we see three metaphors commonly connected with turning to God—waking from sleep, rising from the dead, and living in Christ's light. If you like to draw, illustrate one of these in the space below:

THURSDAY: SPIRIT-FILLED LIVING

1. Pray for wisdom and read the passage we'll be studying today:

Ephesians 5:15 Therefore be very careful how you live—not as unwise but as wise, **5:16** taking advantage of every opportunity, because the days are evil. **5:17** For this reason do not be foolish, but be wise by understanding what the Lord's will is. **5:18** And do not get drunk with wine, which is debauchery, but be filled by the Spirit, **5:19** speaking to one another in psalms, hymns, and spiritual songs, singing and making music in your hearts to the Lord, **5:20** always giving thanks to God the Father for each other in the name of our Lord Jesus Christ, **5:21** and submitting to one another out of reverence for Christ.

2. Therefore. That's how Paul begins v. 15. What's it there for? That is, what was he talking about previously that serves as the reasoning behind his charge to live wisely?

_____

3. In the short space of two verses, Paul gives four imperatives for what wise living looks like. What are they (vv. 15–16)?

_____

_____

4. What is the command given in v. 18?

_____

5. What are the four ways Paul's readers are supposed to live out that command?

- S_____

- S_____ and Making _____

- G_____

- S_____

6. Circle references to "one another" or "each other" in this section found amidst the four imperatives.

7. Paul envisions beautiful lives transformed by the Spirit.

    a. What three kinds of speaking does Paul encourage (v. 19)?

_____

_____

    b. How can you make music in your heart (v. 19)?

_____

_____

    c. For whom are you thankful? Tell God (v. 20)!

_____

_____

    d. Who needs you to serve them out of reverence for Christ, and how will you do so (v. 21)?

_____

8. Once again, Paul says "therefore." Because the days are evil, he wants his readers to live wisely. What are the ways he wants them to demonstrate wise living (vv. 16, 17)?

_____

_____

"Taking advantage of every opportunity" (v. 16)—Or "making the most of the time" (NIV). The metaphor Paul uses here is actually "redeeming" the time (KJV). He says the same thing in Colossians 4:5. Time is a resource we can squander by living unwisely. Since the days are evil and time is short, he exhorts readers to spend time wisely. God's will is our sanctification (1 Thess. 4:3); we must live wisely seeking to conform to God's desire for our time.

9. Ask the Spirit's help and examine how you spend time. In what ways can you better spend it living wisely? What are some things you need to spend more time doing? What do you need to spend less time doing?

FRIDAY: SINGING AND SUBMISSION

1. Pray for wisdom, and read today's text:

Ephesians 5:18 And do not get drunk with wine, which is debauchery, but be filled by the Spirit **5:19** speaking to one another in psalms, hymns, and spiritual songs, singing and making music in your hearts to the Lord, **5:20** always giving thanks to God the Father for each other in the name of our Lord Jesus Christ, **5:21** and submitting to one another out of reverence for Christ.

5:22 Wives, submit to your husbands as to the Lord, **5:23** because the husband is the head of the wife as also Christ is the head of the church—he himself being the savior of the body. **5:24** But as the church submits to Christ, so also wives should submit to their husbands in everything. **5:25** Husbands, love your wives just as Christ loved the church and gave himself for her **5:26** to sanctify her by cleansing her with the washing of the water by the word, **5:27** so that he may present the church to himself as glorious—not having a stain or wrinkle, or any such blemish, but holy and blameless. **5:28** In the same way husbands ought to love their wives as their own bodies. He who loves his wife loves himself. **5:29** For no one has ever hated his own body but he feeds it and takes care of it, just as Christ also does the church, **5:30** for we are members of his body. **5:31** For this reason a man will leave his father and mother and will be joined to his wife, and the two will become one flesh. **5:32** This mystery is great—but I am actually speaking with reference to Christ and the church. **5:33** Nevertheless, each one of you must also love his own wife as he loves himself, and the wife must respect her husband.

"Love" (vv. 25, 28, 33)—There are different words for different kinds of love in the original Greek. The word used for love throughout this passage is not the affectionate kind (*phileo*), but the self-sacrificing, self-giving kind (*agape*). Such love might include affection, but it is more often associated with the kind of loyal covenant love that sacrifices for the unlovely, washes an invalid, changes diapers on people of all ages, and lays down one's life for another.

Paul sometimes wrote long sentences in Greek that would contain more than 90 words. (In the short Book of Ephesians, Paul has eight super-long sentences.) In English we aim for an average of about fifteen or so words per sentence. That's why when we translate, we add a lot of commas, semi-colons, dashes and periods to make the written-in-Greek concepts readily understandable in English. (Plus, in the sixteenth century, people added chapter and verse numbering that were not in the Greek, either, to break up those long sections.) But one challenge created by such additions is that they can subtly alter Paul's emphases. (Such challenges are present in translation of any kind.)

The sentence in Ephesians 5 that Paul begins with "Do not get drunk with wine" (v. 18) is a clear example of such a long sentence. Notice in the NET Bible translation from Sunday of this week's study that verse 22, which falls mid-sentence in Greek, not only begins a new sentence in English, but it's even translated as if it begins a new paragraph. Yet as you can see in my more "wooden" translation below that retains Paul's structure, the word "submit" does not even appear, but is implied:

> **5:18** And do not get drunk with wine, which is debauchery, but be filled by the Spirit
>
> **5:19** speaking to one another in psalms, hymns, and spiritual songs, singing and making music in your hearts to the Lord,

5:20 always giving thanks to God the Father for each other in the name of our Lord Jesus Christ,

5:21 and submitting to one another out of reverence for Christ,

5:22 wives to your husbands as to the Lord, **5:23** because the husband is the head of the wife as also Christ is the head of the church—he himself being the savior of the body. **5:24** But as the church submits to Christ, so also wives should submit to their husbands in everything. **5:25** Husbands, love your wives just as Christ loved the church and gave himself for her **5:26** to sanctify her by cleansing her with the washing of the water by the word, **5:27** so that he may present the church to himself as glorious—not having a stain or wrinkle, or any such blemish, but holy and blameless. **5:28** In the same way husbands ought to love their wives as their own bodies. He who loves his wife loves himself. **5:29** For no one has ever hated his own body but he feeds it and takes care of it, just as Christ also does the church, **5:30** for we are members of his body. **5:31** For this reason a man will leave his father and mother and will be joined to his wife, and the two will become one flesh. **5:32** This mystery is great—but I am actually speaking with reference to Christ and the church. **5:33** Nevertheless, each one of you must also love his own wife as he loves himself, and the wife must respect her husband.

Notice that the marriage Paul has in view is rooted in being filled with the Spirit (v. 18). And he gives specific instruction to wives (vv. 22–25) and husbands (vv. 25–31) within the context of talking about how all believers live Spirit-filled lives (v. 18ff), one evidence of which is submitting to one another (v. 21ff). So, as a subset of all believers submitting to one another, we find husbands and wives filled with the Spirit serving one another.

2. Look at the implied command to the wife (v. 22) and the direct command to the husband (v. 25). What is the directive for her? What is the command assigned to him?

To her:

To him:

3. Is "head" as Paul uses it in this passage (v. 23) a verb or a noun (circle one)?

4. Paul says the husband is head of the wife as Christ is head of the church—He himself being the savior of the body (v. 23). Notice that Paul clarifies and qualifies how he is using the word "head" and in what way the husband is like Christ. Fill in the blanks that show the parallel ideas he is setting forth in v. 23:

Husband = Head of the _____
Christ = Head of the _____
[Christ] Himself = _____ of the _____

5. Notice how Paul uses "savior" as a synonym or equivalent to "head" (an "appositive" in English grammar). Because "head" in English does not have the nuance of "savior," it's difficult for us to see them as equivalent. To help yourself visualize what he means, use your answers in question 4 to help you identify what the head is and what the body is in each of his three pairings. In each diagram below, label the head and the body according to what Paul says each represents.

6. Elsewhere, Paul describes Christ as being head over the church. In such contexts, we find words like "preeminence" and "authority" (e.g., Eph. 1:22). But when Paul uses the preposition "of"h with head as in head of the church, the word "head" appears with the word "body" and/or savior nearby. And instead of "authority" and "preeminence," we find words in such contexts that relate to human bodies, like "grows" and "ligaments" (4:16), "feed," and "take care of" (5:29). "Head over" is a power picture, but "head of" is a oneness picture—a picture Paul is presenting in Ephesians 5. He even quotes Genesis about two becoming one flesh (5:31). The following are some

ways in which Christ is head over and head of the church. Circle the verbs you find describing Christ in this passage, and put the verse reference next to them:

> Christ is the Savior who gave Himself
> Christ is all powerful
> Christ is in control
> Christ is everywhere
> Christ shows sacrificial love for and cares for His Bride
> Christ knows all
> Christ bathes/cleanses the church
> Christ is united in oneness with His bride

7. For the sake of careful study, let's delete the paragraph division, the period, and the added verb that aren't in the original so we can take a closer look at what Paul actually said to wives:

> Be filled with the Spirit...
> submitting to one another out of reverence for Christ,
> wives to your husbands as to the Lord...

"Submitting . . . wives to your husbands as to the Lord" (v. 22)—As noted, wives are to submit as an application of mutual submission of all believers to each other as they are filled with the Spirit. So clearly, it's not a hierarchical organization chart. The husband and wife are equals, but they choose to serve one another as if the other were more important. And the way wives give to the needs of their husbands is with the same attitude with which they serve the Lord.

The word submit carries so much baggage that perhaps it's helpful to begin by clarifying what submission does not mean. First, submission here is not a role; it's an action a woman practices in her role as a wife. And when Paul instructs wives, he makes clear that he wants them to submit to their own husbands, not all men, precisely because he is speaking in the context of a role wives may take on, not all women in general. Additionally, submission is not giving up all efforts to influence the husband; giving in to his every demand; pretending he's better at something when he isn't; automatically deferring to him to make the final decisions in the relationship (see 1 Cor. 7:5); enabling or tolerating abuse; cooperating in sin (see Sapphira in Acts 5), especially when it endangers life (see Abigail in 1 Samuel 25). And finally, submission is not the sum total of what a wife is to be. Submission is love in service to another.

8. If you are married, how can you serve your husband in the power of the Spirit in order to be united with him and for your "entire body" to reach maturity?

_____

_____

"Submit . . . in everything" (v. 23)—It's easy to read Paul's words here and think he intends for a wife to do whatever her husband says, even if he tells her to lie, cheat, and steal. But the death of Sapphira, who cooperated in sin with her husband, should tell us that is not at all what Paul has in mind. First, we must bear in mind that Paul is giving instruction that fits his head/body metaphor. What if a body in the drawing above becomes disconnected from its physical head? How would that fit the oneness image?

The immediate context suggests exactly what Paul means by "everything." His use is similar to how we use the phrase today. A party planner might say, "I'll take care of everything," and we understand this to mean he or she is limiting the meaning to the scope of the party; or a parent might tell a child, "Do everything the babysitter tells you," but it is understood that if the sitter decides to make prank phone calls, the child is not expected to comply.

In Paul's metaphor, the body must submit to the head in all things because they are physically connected—just like Christ and the church are connected, as seen in the previous chapter of Ephesians. The marriage Paul describes is one in which the husband has his wife's welfare constantly in view. The goal is oneness. Together they serve one another, and the result is the growth and flourishing of the entire body—something greater than their individual parts.

9. In what way were husbands to love their wives (v. 25)?

_____

"Cleansing, washing, stain, wrinkle, blemish (spot)" (vv. 26–27)—Interestingly enough, the husband's "cleansing" of his wife is described in laundry terms. Paul again challenges manliness stereotypes to speak of the humility and service the husband is to offer his wife as he seeks her flourishing maturity in the faith. (Imagine what a shock this would have been to Paul's readers!) The idea is not that he is her spiritual teacher or priest, but that he loves her as if she is his own body. If he gets cold, he puts on warmer clothes. If he's exhausted, he goes to sleep. If he's hungry, he eats. He cares for his body because he loves himself. And that is how he is to care for her. As Christ cares for the church, the husband is to seek his wife's good and her growth; an investment in her is an investment in himself, because they are one.

Paul cites Genesis on marriage: "A man will leave his father and mother and will be joined to his wife, and the two will become one flesh" (v. 32; Genesis 2:24). "One" is Paul's consistent word for marriage and his consistent idea throughout the Book of Ephesians: One new man (Jew and Gentile); the body (church) connected to her head (Christ); and the head/body analogy of husband and wife. Can you see it?

Love and respect (5:33)—The apostle Paul summarizes (v. 33), reminding the Spirit-filled husband to sacrificially love and the wife to respect (he seems to be using "respect" as a synonym for submission). The husband is to love his wife sacrificially, even if she is unlovable. The wife is called, as an act of Christ-worship to respect her husband, even if he is undeserving. Such loving and respecting make for perfect symmetry, possible only with the help of the Holy Spirit. Christ died for us when we were his enemies. And the Spirit enables us to do what would be impossible in our flesh.

SATURDAY: HEAD AND BODY

Scripture: The husband is the head of the wife as also Christ is the head of the church—he himself being the savior of the body (Eph. 5:23).

Interestingly enough, when describing the husband, Paul never uses the word "headship." Or "leadership." Or "lead." In both English and Greek, the text says "head." But in English, we use "head" as a verb and a noun: "I head a committee" is "head" as a verb. But in Koine Greek "head" is only a noun—a thing, never a verb. And in Ephesians 5 it means the body part.

We often hear that Paul teaches husbands to lead, but the biblical command is not to lead but to "love"—of the *agapē* variety. We see distortions of Paul in certain Christian media about how the Bible suggests women are made mostly for love and men made mostly for respect. Men and women need both. Love without respect is patronizing.

In saying that women need only love, such authors usually mean *philēo* (i.e., affection, warmth), but when Paul commands husbands to love, he uses the word for the kind of love that means sacrifice (*agapē*) . . . the hard kind—the kind that looks a lot like submission by another name.

Paul never warns against husbands being overbearing or abdicating authority—the two extremes of leadership. His concern is self-focused living versus sacrificial living. In conclusion, he commands husbands to love sacrificially, to nurture their wives, because their wives are their own selves, connected at the neck.

The wife submits because the husband is "head." And in this use of "head," the head and body are a metaphor; "head" is something the husband is in the picture, not something he is to do or become. A body comes under (literally) a head when it's attached. To use horrible grammar: He are her and she are him. They are one.

Sexual intercourse is a horizontal picture of two becoming one; but the head and body connected is a vertical picture of two becoming one. And the Bible's consistent teaching on marriage from the beginning is that two become one,

Paul's teaching on marriage is this: Husband, love your wife as yourself because "she are you," attached at the neck. Nurture and cherish her because you two are one. Wife, you're connected to the head as the body in this metaphor. So be united with that head. You are physically under the head, but not in the sense that an assistant is under a boss in an organization chart. The body metaphor is not at all about rank—though we have often made it so. The options are only oneness or an ugly beheading. That may sound dramatic, but consider how serious this makes marriage to Paul. The destruction of a marriage is not getting rid of a boss or assistant and replacing him or her. It is the separation of a head from its body, making two parts of what is one living organism. It dies by being torn apart, and such a death is a completely unideal state for this union—not God's beautiful design for his creatures.

What's the point of all this? It's actually not marriage. It's about something marriage models that all believers are part of—Christ and the church. So, whether or not you are married, you are part of the image. The wife models the church, serving Christ in love; the husband models Christ, giving up his will for another to the point of death in love. If you are in the church, you are a "body part" that collectively makes up the body connected to Christ as head. You are united with Him in love; and you are loved by Him. Christ in love left heaven, enrobed Himself in humanity in service, and ultimately gave His life for you. Nothing in the world gives you more worth than that. Remember this and give thanks.

For Memorization: "Therefore, be imitators of God as dearly loved children" (Eph. 5:1).

Prayer: *Heavenly Father, thank you for your Son, the church's living Head. Thank you that in Him we have been made alive in newness of life. Thank you for bringing your children from the kingdom of darkness into the kingdom of your beloved Son. Thank you for shining light in our darkness. Help us to walk in the light. To live wisely. To redeem the time. To speak kindly. To give thanks for all the things and people you have given. You have given so very much. Thank you. In Jesus' name, Amen.*

Week 6 of 6

Equipped: Ephesians 6

In the first half of the Book of Ephesians, the apostle Paul laid out the Christian's new identity in Christ. In the second half, he provides the "so what," or the ramifications. As he outlines what Spirit-filled living looks like (Eph. 5:18ff), he envisions a community in which people show Christ's love by serving one another. And one of the places where such service happens is in the household—where we would have found spouses, kids, and their slaves.

People living in the first century Roman Empire would have been familiar with instructions known as "household codes." These codes outlined the ideal for life in the household, and such instructions were always addressed only to the husband. Consider this sample of household-code instruction from Aristotle (384–322 B.C.):

> Of household management we have seen that there are three parts–one is the rule of a master over slaves . . . another of a father, and the third of a husband. A husband and father, we saw, rules over wife and children, both free, but the rule differs, the rule over his children being a royal, over his wife a constitutional rule. . . . The rule of a father

over his children is royal, for he rules by virtue both of love and of the respect due to age, exercising a kind of royal power (Aristotle, *Politics*, Book 1, XII).

The codes' influence was so great that emperors passed laws establishing them as the rule of the land. People who followed them were perceived as upholding civic values. Before Paul's time, Hellenistic synagogues had borrowed the codes' outline as a testimony to the outside world. And the apostle Peter, Paul's contemporary, did so as well. In their view, the Christians' familial life was to match if not exceed the best of Greco-Roman ideals. (For examples, see Eph. 5:22–6:9; Col. 3:18–4:1; 1 Tim. 2:9–15; Titus 2: 2–10; and 1 Pet. 2: 13–3: 7).

Their adaptations require careful observation, however. In the common understanding, a free man reigned unilaterally as king in his home, served by his wife, children, and slaves; in Paul's subtly subversive remix, the male householder was to serve to the point of laying down his life. Paul's genius is in providing countercultural advice in a way that upholds cultural ideals, making it more difficult for critics to accuse Christians of being a threat to society.

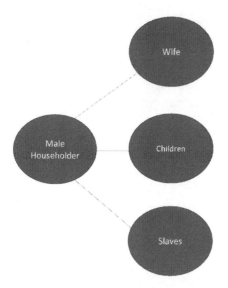

Looking closely, we see that one of Paul's innovations is to elevate the vulnerable by speaking directly to the less powerful family members; he addresses instruction specifically to wives, children, and even slaves, none of whom are ever addressed in secular household codes.

He even speaks to them first in each pairing (wife/husband; children/father; slave/master).

And whereas people like Aristotle expected husbands to rule, Paul tells husbands to serve to the point of sacrifice, even to the point of enduring violence. A man was considered manly in Paul's day if he did not have to experience anyone touching his body without consent. Slaves, gladiators, soldiers, and non-citizens had no such rights. Imagine the surprise to readers, then, when Paul suggested that husbands should offer up their bodies—citing Jesus as the ultimate example. Paul is basically telling these men to sacrifice their man-card if necessary in order to serve others.

In borrowing the structure, Paul is not saying slavery is okay. He's simply following the expected literary structure while radically modifying it to show the importance of humility and service as evidence of Spirit-filled living. In borrowing but repurposing, Paul creates a Christian innovation. He appears to be upholding society's structures, yet his major adaptations infuse the codes with upside-down gospel values.

He does all this because Christians serve a humble master who came not to be served, but to serve and to give up his life for others. We are to die to self, daily.

Who needs your humble service? Do you need to push back against cultural expectations, including some gender norms, if necessary for the sake of the gospel?

MONDAY: FAMILY LIFE AND EQUIPMENT FOR BATTLE

1. Pray for the Spirit's insight and read the last chapter of Ephesians.

Ephesians 6:1: Children, obey your parents in the Lord for this is right. **6:2 "Honor your father and mother,"** which is the first commandment accompanied by a promise, namely, **6:3 "that it may go well with you and that you will live a long time on the earth."**

6:4 Fathers, do not provoke your children to anger, but raise them up in the discipline and instruction of the Lord.

6:5 Slaves, obey your human masters with fear and trembling, in the sincerity of your heart as to Christ, **6:6** not like those who do their work only when someone is watching—as people-pleasers—but as slaves of Christ doing the will of God from the heart. **6:7** Obey with enthusiasm, as though serving the Lord and not people, **6:8**

because you know that each person, whether slave or free, if he does something good, this will be rewarded by the Lord.

6:9 Masters, treat your slaves the same way, giving up the use of threats, because you know that both you and they have the same master in heaven, and there is no favoritism with him.

6:10 Finally, be strengthened in the Lord and in the strength of his power. **6:11** Clothe yourselves with the full armor of God so that you may be able to stand against the schemes of the devil. **6:12** For our struggle is not against flesh and blood, but against the rulers, against the powers, against the world rulers of this darkness, against the spiritual forces of evil in the heavens. **6:13** For this reason, take up the full armor of God so that you may be able to stand your ground on the evil day, and having done everything, to stand. **6:14** Stand firm therefore, by fastening the belt of truth around your waist, by putting on the breastplate of righteousness, **6:15** by fitting your feet with the preparation that comes from the good news of peace, **6:16** and in all of this, by taking up the shield of faith with which you can extinguish all the flaming arrows of the evil one. **6:17** And take the **helmet of salvation** and the sword of the Spirit, which is the word of God. **6:18** With every prayer and petition, pray at all times in the Spirit, and to this end be alert, with all perseverance and requests for all the saints. **6:19** Pray for me also, that I may be given the message when I begin to speak—that I may confidently make known the mystery of the gospel, **6:20** for which I am an ambassador in chains. Pray that I may be able to speak boldly as I ought to speak.

6:21 Tychicus, my dear brother and faithful servant in the Lord, will make everything known to you, so that you too may know about my circumstances, how I am doing. **6:22** I have sent him to you for this very purpose, that you may know our circumstances and that he may encourage your hearts.

6:23 Peace to the brothers and sisters, and love with faith, from God the Father and the Lord Jesus Christ. **6:24** Grace be with all of those who love our Lord Jesus Christ with an undying love.

2. What did you notice in particular? Does anything especially address something you're going through or call you to a higher standard? What does Paul seem to be emphasizing?

1. Pray for wisdom and read the passage for today's study:

> **Ephesians 6:1** Children, obey your parents in the Lord for this is right. **6:2 "Honor your father and mother,"** which is the first commandment accompanied by a promise, namely, **6:3 "that it may go well with you and that you will live a long time on the earth."**
>
> **6:4** Fathers, do not provoke your children to anger, but raise them up in the discipline and instruction of the Lord.
>
> **6:5** Slaves, obey your human masters with fear and trembling, in the sincerity of your heart as to Christ, **6:6** not like those who do their work only when someone is watching—as people-pleasers—but as slaves of Christ doing the will of God from the heart. **6:7** Obey with enthusiasm, as though serving the Lord and not people, **6:8** because you know that each person, whether slave or free, if he does something good, this will be rewarded by the Lord.
>
> **6:9** Masters, treat your slaves the same way, giving up the use of threats, because you know that both you and they have the same master in heaven, and there is no favoritism with him.

Notice the bold typeface on verses 2 and 3? That tells us Paul is quoting the Old Testament. In this case, he's going back to Mt. Sinai, where Moses received the Ten Commandments. We read the story in Exodus 20. And the specific wording there is found in v. 12:

> "Honor your father and your mother, that you may live a long time in the land the Lord your God is giving to you."

Compare it with the paraphrase in Ephesians 6:1–3:

> Children, obey your parents in the Lord for this is right. "Honor your father and mother," which is the first commandment accompanied by a promise, namely, "that it may go well with you and that you will live a long time on the earth."

2. How do the two passages differ? Notice how Paul generalizes the wording of the fifth commandment to disconnect the benefit from the Promised Land and apply it to Gentiles.

_____

_____

"Obey . . . in the Lord" (v. 1)—Paul amps up the language from "honor" (always true of offspring to parents) to "obey" (temporarily true in childhood of offspring to parents). He is not saying all children must obey all orders from all parents. Remember, he has in view a household full of Spirit-filled Christians ("in the Lord").

Paul also observes that "Honor your father and mother," one of the Ten Commandments, is accompanied by a cause/effect relationship: length of life. In Moses's day, the people were wandering in the wilderness on their way to the land God promised them. And God made a contract with Israel that if the nation obeyed while in that land, they would succeed; if they disobeyed, they would suffer. (The promise was generalized, not individualized) And the cause-and-effect relationship between obedience to parents and long life is still generally true. There is a true benefit to Spirit-filled children obeying righteous parents.

3. We never outgrow the responsibility to honor our parents, and our doing so models for kids how to treat our elders. What are some ways we can honor our parents at various stages of the life cycle?

Having addressed children, Paul continues following the outline of household codes, addressing the paterfamilias or householder. And he writes:

> "Fathers, do not provoke your children to anger, but raise them up in the discipline and instruction of the Lord."

The addressees could be understood as "parents" rather than "fathers," but because of the household-code structure, most translators think Paul probably means to say "fathers," even if the instruction applies to both. A Christian parent's number-one job is not to bring up children terrified of ever doing anything wrong, but in the discipline and instruction of the Lord.

4. If you are a parent, what are some ways your children need you to discipline and instruct them in love?

---

5. If you are not a parent, what are some ways you can nurture and guide in the faith your nieces, nephews, godchildren, Sunday school kids...?

_____

_____

Having given children and parents instructions, Paul turns to the slave/master relationship. Often in the twenty-first century we read verses about slaves and immediately apply them to employment contexts. Yet slaves and employees are not really parallel. Slaves were owned by their masters. They didn't get evenings and weekends off. They didn't have boundaries between work and private life. They lived under the same roof. And in some unbelieving homes, they had to be available sexually to their masters, whether male or female. The slave and master were not equals.

Conversely, bosses and employees are equal, but employees choose to submit for the sake of earning money—yet they can legally walk off the job. Slaves had no such rights. Thus, they did not submit (serve as equals)—they obeyed (serving as the lower-ranking person in a hierarchy).

6. Circle references to slaves serving the Lord/as to Christ/of Christ (vv. 5–7). Do you see the emphasis?

7. With what attitude are righteous slaves to serve their masters (v. 5)?

_____

_____

8. What contrast does Paul give for how slaves are and are not to act (v. 6–7)? What was the will of God for them?

_____

_____

9. What hope does Paul offer them, even if they are not rewarded by masters for rendering enthusiastic service (v. 8)?

_____

10. Although slaves are not employees, if people in bondage could serve with such attitudes, how much more should employees do so. If you are in a position of vocational service, how can you serve in winsome, counter-cultural ways?

_____

_____

11. What does Paul tell masters (which could be male or female) to give up, and why?

_____

12. Paul grounds his advice in the character of God. What does he say is true of God? Why should that matter to any Christian in a position of authority?

_____

WEDNESDAY: THE ARMOR OF GOD

1. Pray for insight. Then read the following:

> **Ephesians 6:10** Finally, be strengthened in the Lord and in the strength of his power. **6:11** Clothe yourselves with the full armor of God so that you may be able to stand against the schemes of the devil. **6:12** For our struggle is not against flesh and blood, but against the rulers, against the powers, against the world rulers of this darkness, against the spiritual forces of evil in the heavens. **6:13** For this reason, take up the full armor of God so that you may be able to stand your ground on the evil day, and having done everything,

to stand. **6:14** Stand firm therefore, by fastening the belt of truth around your waist, by putting on the breastplate of righteousness, **6:15** by fitting your feet with the preparation that comes from the good news of peace, **6:16** and in all of this, by taking up the shield of faith with which you can extinguish all the flaming arrows of the evil one. **6:17** And take the **helmet of salvation** and the sword of the Spirit, which is the word of God. **6:18** With every prayer and petition, pray at all times in the Spirit, and to this end be alert, with all perseverance and requests for all the saints.

In 16 B.C. Rome was so full of people selling powers that all the magicians were expelled from the city. Years later, the Roman emperor Vespasian outlawed astrology in the empire, too. Yet because of his friendship with a famous Ephesian astrologer, Balbillus, Vespasian allowed Ephesus to continue holding "sacred" games in Balbillus's honor.

In the Book of Acts we find a story set in first-century Ephesus about magicians who convert to Christianity (Acts 19:19). They bring out their expensive magic books and build a "bonfire of the vanities" with them. (Note the difference between choosing to burn your own books and having someone confiscate them against your will.)

This happened in a context in which Artemis of the Ephesians was believed to be powerful enough to overcome the astrological world. When I photographed her first-century statue some years ago, I noticed the signs of the zodiac inscribed on her chest. And a statue of Hecate, the goddess of the underworld, stood in her temple. One theory as to why Artemis's "legs" are covered with animals is that she was considered to have power over anything in the earthly realm, including human and beast.

Thanks to Artemis worship, Ephesus was a center of commerce for people trafficking in the supernatural. Magicians could charge a lot for love potions. Or people would give magicians large sums to create curses using a combination of the "Ephesian letters." Mentioned in the introduction to this study, these were probably a set of letters that people had inscribed in leather that they would use like dice in varying combinations for spells.

Scholar Clinton E. Arnold sees a connection between the city of Ephesus's reputation for the demonic and the Book of Ephesians, which includes the only extended section in the New Testament about how to arm oneself against the dark powers. The presence of supernatural evil would also explain why "power" as a motif keeps showing up in this letter—starting in chapter 1.

2. Paul begins his conclusion with another reference to power: "Finally, be strengthened in the Lord and in the strength of his power" (v. 10). He is emphatic about the source, stating it twice for emphasis. In whose strength do we change?

---

3. We have a strong enemy, but our God is stronger. Yet we cannot stand by passively; we must take action. In the passage below, circle all the references to standing, every occurrence of the word "all," and every imperative.

> **Ephesians 6:11** Clothe yourselves with the full armor of God so that you may be able to stand against the schemes of the devil. **6:12** For our struggle is not against flesh and blood, but against the rulers, against the powers, against the world rulers of this darkness, against the spiritual forces of evil in the heavens. **6:13** For this reason, take up the full armor of God so that you may be able to stand your ground on the evil day, and having done everything, to stand. **6:14** Stand firm therefore, by fastening the belt of truth around your waist, by putting on the breastplate of righteousness, **6:15** by fitting your feet with the preparation that comes from the good news of peace, **6:16** and in all of this, by taking up the shield of faith with which you can extinguish all the flaming arrows of the evil one. **6:17** And take the helmet of salvation and the sword of the Spirit, which is the word of God. **6:18** With every prayer and petition, pray at all times in the Spirit, and to this end be alert, with all perseverance and requests for all the saints.

4. Fill in the chart so you can see Paul's emphasis (not all boxes will be filled):

Verses	Do this	Why or how	Result
v. 11–12			
vv. 13–12			
v. 14			
v. 16			
vv. 17			
v. 18			

"Flesh and blood" (v. 12)—In other words, we are not actually struggling against humans, but rather the forces of darkness that war against us.

5. What words does Paul use to describe the forces of darkness (vv. 11–12)?

_____

6. List some examples of when you have fallen for the evil one's schemes, whether through interpersonal conflict, lying to cover yourself, or doubting the goodness of God.

_____

_____

7. Notice that Paul does not tell his readers to flee, but to stand. The only time he tells readers to flee is when it comes to sexual immorality (1 Cor. 6:18). The rest of the time we are to arm ourselves with spiritual weapons and go on the offensive as warriors. Paul fully believes that when properly adorned with spiritual weapons, we can stand firm. Look at the chart on the following page. What constitutes the full armor?

Belt =
Breastplate =
Footwear =
Shield =
Helmet =
Sword of the Spirit =
All this weaponry is covered in prayer.

8. Go through the mental exercise of putting on your armor. Pray for yourself and your family and your church that you will stand strong.

In the Book of Ephesians, we find Christ presented as supreme and exalted, which would have comforted believers coming out of the occult and fearing what the powers of evil might do to them. Paul assures his readers about their new identity—that of new citizens transplanted from the dark kingdom to the kingdom of light. He describes them as sharers in divine power through faith, and he describes the evil order as led by the enslaving "prince of the authority of the air." Although Paul acknowledges the continuing power of evil, he assures believers that ultimately all powers will be subjected to Christ. A day is coming when we can lay down our weapons and celebrate the victory. Give thanks!

> **Christian Fiction with Spiritual Warfare Themes**
> *The Screwtape Letters*, by C. S. Lewis
> The Space Trilogy of novels, by C. S. Lewis
> *Descent into Hell*, by Charles Williams
> *A Swiftly Tilting Planet*, by Madeleine L'Engle
> *This Present Darkness*, by Frank Peretti
> *The Tutor's First Love*, by George MacDonald
> *The Zeal of Thy House*, by Dorothy Sayers

THURSDAY: BOLDNESS TO SHARE THE GOSPEL

1. Pray for insight. Then read the verses for today:

> **Ephesians 6:19** Pray for me also, that I may be given the message when I begin to speak—that I may confidently make known

the mystery of the gospel, **6:20** for which I am an ambassador in chains. Pray that I may be able to speak boldly as I ought to speak.

2. Paul, stuck in an underground prison, had every reason to despair. Yet his priorities were the spread of the gospel. He saw himself as an ambassador in chains. Think about that for a moment—ambassadors are official envoys, sometimes high-ranking diplomats, who represent their homes while living on foreign soil. Paul was a Roman citizen residing in Rome. Yet he called himself an ambassador. What does this tell you about how Paul viewed his citizenship?

_____

3. What was Paul's main prayer request, emphasized in several ways?

_____

4. His concern was the furtherance of the gospel, not his personal comfort. He saw his circumstances as an opportunity to proclaim the secret now revealed—that God had mercy on the Gentiles. People had betrayed him, falsely accused him, stalked him to bring him to ruin—yet he referred to the results of their injustice as an embassy assignment. That is undying love for Christ! What are some of your "embassy assignments"?

_____

_____

5. Paul adds an interesting word: "ought" (v. 20). He says he ought to speak boldly. Why do you think he views boldness as an obligation?

_____

6. Who do you know that needs Jesus Christ? Pray for this person that God would create an open heart and give you opportunity to speak of His beauty. Pray for those having a gospel witness both in your community and across the world.

Maybe you wonder how to share the gospel. It's pretty simple. You share that Christ died and Christ arose along with the ramifications of these two great historical events. His burial was evidence of His death; His appearing to many people was the evidence of His resurrection (see 1 Cor. 15). And the rest of what you share is what it all means. God designed a beautiful world, but all have sinned; we need a Savior to restore us to peace with God; Christ took our place in bearing the consequences of our sin; He died and rose, conquering death; now believe and receive him. Tell your story.

7. Pray for yourself the things Paul asked his readers to pray—that you'll be given the message (notice in verse 19 that he has to start speaking before the message arrives), deliver it with confidence, and speak boldly.

FRIDAY: TYCHICUS

1. Pray for insight. Then read the final verses in Ephesians 6:

> **Ephesians 6:21** Tychicus, my dear brother and faithful servant in the Lord, will make everything known to you, so that you too may know about my circumstances, how I am doing. **6:22** I have sent him to you for this very purpose, that you may know our circumstances and that he may encourage your hearts.
>
> **6:23** Peace to the brothers and sisters, and love with faith, from God the Father and the Lord Jesus Christ. **6:24** Grace be with all of those who love our Lord Jesus Christ with an undying love.

2. How does Paul describe Tychicus (v. 21)?

_____

3. Circle all the references to Paul, the prisoner, thinking of others rather than himself (vv. 21–22).

4. On the map provided, draw the route by boat from Rome to Ephesus, then by land from Ephesus to Colossae.

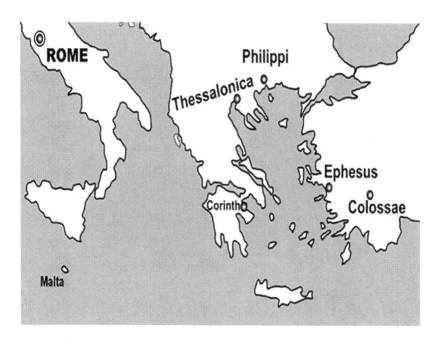

As far as we know, Paul was writing from a prison cell in Rome. And he sent his co-worker Tychicus to Colossae to deliver three missives: what are known to us as the New Testament books of Colossians, Philemon (its recipient also lived in Colossae), and Ephesians. As mentioned, the latter was probably intended also for the church at Laodicea, which lay a short distance north of Colossae. If you trace the route Tychicus would have taken by boat from Rome (see map), you'll observe that he probably would have sailed to Ephesus. From there he could have walked about 100 miles due east to Laodicea, and then traveled a short distance to Colossae.

Accompanying Tychicus was a runaway slave, Onesimus, whom Paul had led to Christ. After helping Onesimus grow as a believer, Paul sent him accompanied by Tychicus back to his owner, Philemon. With Onesimus, Paul sent a letter asking Philemon, a fellow believer, to welcome Onesimus as a brother, even though Philemon had the right by law to kill him for running away.

We know that Tychicus was originally from Asia (Acts 20:4) and had gone to Macedonia with Paul after the great Ephesian riot that prompted him to leave Ephesus (19:34–20:1); if so, Tychicus would have experienced some danger to himself. Tychicus had gone all the way to Rome with Paul, and now he was returning to his home province.

Two of Paul's three letters sent in the same pouch speak of Tychicus:

"Tychicus, my dear brother and faithful servant in the Lord, will make everything known to you, so that you too may know about my circumstances, how I am doing" (Eph. 6:21).

"Tychicus, a dear brother, faithful minister, and fellow slave in the Lord, will tell you all the news about me" (Col. 4:7).

About four years later, Paul writes to Titus in Crete, "When I send Artemas or Tychicus to you, do your best to come to me at Nicopolis, for I have decided to spend the winter there" (Titus 3:12).

At the end of Paul's life, he writes to Timothy, "Only Luke is with me. Get Mark and bring him with you, because he is a great help to me in ministry. Now I have sent Tychicus to Ephesus" (2 Tim. 4:11–12).

Putting it all together, throughout Paul's ministry we see Tychicus doing a lot of traveling on the apostle's behalf in and out of the province of Asia. When I toured that region of the world, my guide told me he had mapped out all these routes and marveled that Paul and his friends had walked so many, many miles.

Tychicus is mentioned repeatedly as serving Paul faithfully in the ministry of the gospel over years of service. He is never front-and-center, but he's always there willing to travel hundreds of miles in less-than-ideal conditions, for the sake of the gospel.

The Mamertine Prison in Rome, Italy, in antiquity was called the Tullianum. Today it is open to the public. If you are ever in Rome, why not visit this prison where Paul is said to have been incarcerated? The address is Clivo Argentario, 1, 00186 Roma RM, Italy.

5. Whom do you know who serves faithfully behind the scenes for the sake of the gospel? Write them a note of thanks.

6. Peace, love, faith, and grace have been key themes in the Book of Ephesians. Paul includes all of these in his benediction. Circle them:

"Peace to the brothers and sisters, and love with faith, from God the Father and the Lord Jesus Christ. Grace be with all of those who love our Lord Jesus Christ with an undying love" (6:23-24).

7. Remember how we began with a warning to those in Ephesus about losing their first love? Now Paul closes his wonderful missive with a blessing of grace on those who love our Lord Jesus Christ with an undying love. What obstacles keep you from loving Christ with undying love? What do you see as the biggest threats to your faith? Pray for yourself that you will remain faithful to the end.

SATURDAY: THE STRUGGLE IS REAL

Scripture: "For our struggle is not against flesh and blood, but against the rulers, against the powers, against the world rulers of this darkness, against the spiritual forces of evil in the heavens" (Eph. 6:12).

My friend Angela tells this story:

"What in the world can you possibly offer those people?"

I often uttered those words to myself as I looked in the mirror, questioning why God would call me into ministry and bring me to seminary. But this time, the words did not come from inside my head. A loved one spoke them to me across the dinner table. While I dug my fingernails into my hands to keep from crying, waves of hurt and anger crashed over me. I scanned the restaurant for the closest exit, ready to make a quick escape.

Right as I stood to leave, I remembered all those times in front of the mirror—the exact same words. A Bible verse flashed through my mind: "For our struggle is not against flesh and blood, but against rulers. . . ." And I smiled.

Our enemy, the accuser, is dishonest. Jesus called him a "liar, and the father of lies" (John 8:44). He prowls to see who he can destroy (1 Pet. 5:8).

What lies does the enemy use to attack you? Did you put in long hours and land the account only to be passed over for a promotion? Have God's people betrayed you? Has someone taken credit for your work? Perhaps your neighbor posts Pinterest-worthy dinners and décor, while you struggle to serve grilled cheese. Do the same arguments erupt in your house time and again, with sharp words slashing open old wounds? The pain and shame of these moments can feel like a sucker-punch. And sucker-punch it is—just not from the source we think. They come from our real enemy.

At dinner that night, I remembered God's truth. My struggle was with the enemy of my soul rather than the person in front of me. I recognized the pattern of the lie. I looked at my loved one, and I could forgive him. Although I was hurt through him, I wasn't hurt by him. The attack came from the enemy. The Enemy wanted to hook me with that lie and make me flounder in the enormity of it until I gave up.

Instead of getting caught by the bait, we must remember our fight isn't totally with the person who wounds. Our scuffle is ultimately with the powers we can't see, who do everything they can to take us down.

What are your weak spots? Where are you given to despair? What makes you doubt the goodness of God? What circumstances cause you to distrust his ways? Suit up in the power of the Holy Spirit. Cover everything in prayer. Our weapons are not of this world, and neither are our battles. But we have the power of the risen Christ at our disposal. And we are not alone.

Memorize: "With every prayer and petition, pray at all times in the Spirit, and to this end be alert, with all perseverance and requests for all the saints" (Eph. 6:18).

Prayer: *Father God, grant me the grace to love you more, to gear up and stand strong. Help me not to shrink back, but to run into the war zone equipped in your armor. Help me to see my circumstances through your eyes. Use me to spread the gospel. Thank you for the blessings you have lavished upon your children in Christ. Help me never, no matter what, to stop loving your Son with an undying love. In Christ's name I pray, Amen.*

LEADER'S GUIDE

Do you sense God leading you to facilitate a group? To lead a Coffee Cup Bible study, you do not need a seminary degree or skill at public speaking. You don't even need to have the gift of teaching. You need only a desire to see people grow through God's Word and a genuine concern for their spiritual development. Often the person best suited to the facilitator's role is not someone who likes to impart knowledge (teach). Rather, it's someone who enjoys drawing out others and listening. Begin with prayer, asking the Lord to guide you.

Get Started
Pray about whom you should invite to join you. Then begin inviting participants, and set a deadline for commitments. Ask yourself the best way to communicate to others the opportunity for group study—church bulletin? web site? Facebook group? blog? text? e-mail? flier? poster? phone call?

If you envision a church-sponsored study with a number of small groups, aim to give participants at least several months' notice so you can schedule a room and let participants add the event to their calendars. Work with the appropriate church staff to solidify details of time and place.

If you plan to gather a small group of friends, decide as a group the best time and place to meet. Ideally, small groups should be limited to no more than ten members.

Take book orders, collect payment, and distribute books in advance or have each individual take care of obtaining her own. The former is recommended, however, because bulk discounts are often available; plus, people are more likely to follow through and attend if they already have a book.

Before the first meeting, determine whether to distribute studies in advance or hand them out at your kickoff. You also need to decide if members should read only the background information in the introduction the first week or read the introduction along with completing the first week of study. If the former, plan for how you will fill the time at your first meeting, as you will have little to discuss. Perhaps you can do a service project together, such as writing to a child whom a group member sponsors. Or sharing your own faith story so your group can get to know you. Or letting each person tell her story. Or reading Ephesians aloud as a group. (If someone prefers not to read aloud, have the group read in unison during her turn.)

Something else you'll need to decide: do you want to complete each chapter in one week or spread out your study over a longer period? If the latter, determine where to divide each week's lesson.

Obtain permission to distribute contact information among the members of your group to encourage discussion and fellowship throughout the week. Include phone, e-mail, and street-address information.

Kick It Off

Before your first Bible discussion time, hold a kickoff brunch, or get your group together at church, a coffee shop, or in a home. Pray for each person who will attend, asking that God's presence would be felt and that each woman would have a desire to learn the Word. Open with prayer.

Provide opportunities for members to get acquainted if they don't already know each other. Do this by providing introductions or asking icebreaker questions that include each participant giving her name and some background information. Ask a benign question with the potential for humor. This will help people open up to each other. For example, "What is your favorite timesaving invention?" (Water heater? Lawnmower? Coffeemaker?)

Hold Your First Discussion Meeting

When the group meets for the first discussion, be sure all participants meet each other if they haven't already. Distribute contact information, and be sure everyone has a study book.

You will spend most of your time in discussion. If your group members hardly know each other or seem reluctant to talk, use a prepared icebreaker question to get them started. Try to come up with something that relates to the topic without requiring a spiritual answer. You may have people in your group who are completely uncomfortable talking about spiritual things, and the icebreaker is a way to help them participate in a less-threatening manner. In fact, you might want to include an icebreaker at the beginning of each discussion to get lighthearted conversation going. See the list of suggestions at the end of this chapter for possible questions for each week.

Structure Your Weekly Meeting

Begin each session with prayer, and do your best to start on time, depending on the formality of the group. Set a clear ending time, and respect participants' schedules.

After prayer, ask the icebreaker question, then move to discussion. Plan to allow about forty-five minutes for this time. Select the questions you'll ask by going back through the lesson for the week and choosing about seven open-ended questions. You can simply circle in your book the questions you want to ask. Be sure at least one of your choices covers what you feel is the most important point from the text for that week.

As the leader, you need to be careful not to dominate. Your job is not to instruct but to draw out. If you have a member who rarely says anything, periodically direct an easy question specifically to that person.

When you finish the final question, ask members if there was a question or issue they wanted to cover that you missed. Then ask them to share prayer requests, items for thanksgiving, and announcements. Be sure each request is actually covered in prayer and encourage the group to refrain from answering such requests with advice or related stories ("I know someone else with that kind of cancer, and she used an herbal supplement . . ."). After you are finished taking prayer requests, be sure each person knows the next assignment as well as the meeting time and place for your next study.

Between meetings, pray for participants. It will mean a lot if you can follow up with a phone call, particularly when people have shared urgent requests. If you can make one visit to each person's home while the study is ongoing, you will likely reap huge dividends in the time invested. Just showing up and meeting people where they are goes a long way toward building community and aiding spiritual growth.

Beyond Bible Study

Perhaps you would like to combine your time in Bible study with service. You can choose from the following ways to do so or come up with your own ideas.

Bring something to donate every week. One week, perhaps used eyeglasses. The next, it's cell phones to recycle. Then, used Bibles to go to an organization that distributes them to the needy or in countries where Bibles are not readily available. Finally, bring books to donate to the public library or your church library. Other possibilities are combining your time with a baby shower to benefit a Pregnancy Resource Center or collecting coats for the homeless. Involve the group in deciding what they want to do.

Combine your study with your community's needs or a church's missionary needs. One week, have everyone bring supplies such as energy bars, dried soup, and seeds for someone's ministry trip. Often short-term teams need items to give as gifts to translators as well as for vacation Bible school prizes. My congregation's sister church in Mexico has asked for school supplies in September and for Spanish Bibles. Other possibilities might include bringing blankets and water bottles for the homeless, bringing office and bathroom supplies for a local ministry, or hosting a group garage sale and using the proceeds to grant scholarships for an activity such as an annual women's retreat.

Target a people group or community-service organization to learn about and pray for as part of your time together.

Adopt a missionary of the week or month to correspond with, pray for, and learn about each time you meet.

Choose a group within your community to serve. If a nursing home, visit it together one week and take some large-print Bibles or other books. Or volunteer to pick up trash in an area where your city has a need. Take a fruit basket to your local firefighters. Or deliver meals to shut-ins.

Work together as a group on a craft to donate, such as sewing blankets for a women's shelter (make sure to provide basic training). Local homeless shelters often have ongoing demand for pillowcases and hot pads—which are easy to make. Or learn to knit and donate scarves to the homeless to help them through long winters.

By linking time in God's Word with time serving others, you will help group members move from compartmentalizing to integrating their discipleship time and the stewardship of their resources.

Lists of and links to additional helps for your Bible discussion time are available at aspire2.com in the Coffee Cup Bible Studies section of the site. If your group generates ideas they want to share with others, send them through the contact page on the site. We'd love to know what worked for you.

Perhaps you have some artists or musicians in your group who need more right-brained interaction. Songs, jewelry, paintings, photos, collages, poetry, prayers, psalms—the options for creative interaction in response to the truths learned in Ephesians are endless. Someone might want to come up with a music playlist that will help you learn verses from Ephesians.

Finally, if you are meeting at a coffee shop or restaurant, learn the name of your barista or server and the person cleaning your table. You may be the only people they meet all day who seem to care.

Discussion Starters

Remember that icebreaker questions are simply to get discussion started. When you open with an easy question, everyone should be able to answer. No one should feel intimidated. If you wish, craft questions that better fit your own group.

Week 1, United, Ephesians 1—What's your favorite love story?

Week 2, Reconciled, Ephesians 2—Tell about an unexpected reconciliation. It can be fiction or non-fiction. Perhaps you heard a story in the news or saw it on film or experienced it.

Week 3, Belonging, Ephesians 3—Share a time when someone made you feel welcome.

Week 4, New and Diverse, Ephesians 4—Tell of a time when someone used their gifts to encourage or bless you.

Week 5, Spirit-Filled, Ephesians 5—What's the worst parenting advice you've ever heard? The best?

Week 6, Equipped, Ephesians 6—Share a time when someone gave you excellent customer service.

About the NET BIBLE®

The NET BIBLE® is an exciting new translation of the Bible with 60,932 translators' notes! These translators' notes make the original Greek, Hebrew and Aramaic texts of the Bible far more accessible and unlocks the riches of the Bible's truth from entirely new perspectives.

The NET BIBLE® is the first modern Bible to be completely free for anyone, anywhere in the world to download as part of a powerful new "Ministry First" approach being pioneered at bible.org.

Download the entire NET Bible and
60,932 notes for free at www.bible.org

About the bible.org ministry

Before there was eBay® . . . before there was Amazon.com® . . . there was bible.org! Bible.org is a non-profit (501c3) Christian ministry headquartered in Dallas, Texas. In the last decade bible.org has grown to serve millions of individuals around the world and provides thousands of trustworthy resources for Bible study (2 Tim 2:2).

Go to www.bible.org for thousands
of trustworthy resources including:

- The NET BIBLE®
- Discipleship Materials
- The Theology Program
- More than 10,000 Sermon Illustrations
- ABC's of Christian Growth
- Bible Dictionaries and Commentaries

Made in the USA
Lexington, KY
04 January 2019